Unleashing Resilience

thriving in the crucible

Discover inspiring real-life stories of individuals who encountered insurmountable obstacles and setbacks but demonstrated the bravery and resilience to overcome them.

By the author of Destiny's Kaleidoscope

Vikas Parihar

ISBN 979-8-89233-381-8

“
WITHIN THE STORMS OF RESILIENCE,
WE UNEARTH THE UNBREAKABLE SPIRIT„

Contents

Prologue

In the pages of this book, we will explore real-life examples of individuals who have faced unimaginable challenges and setbacks, yet found the courage and resilience to rise above them. From entrepreneurs who turned failures into success stories to athletes who defied the odds to achieve greatness, their stories will inspire and motivate you to embrace your own resilience.

We will also delve into the science behind resilience, understanding the psychological and emotional factors that contribute to our ability to bounce back from adversity. Through expert insights and research, you will gain a deeper understanding of how resilience can be cultivated and strengthened.

Each chapter will be a journey of self-discovery, guiding you through exercises and reflections to tap into your inner resilience. You will learn practical strategies to build resilience in your daily life, empowering you to face challenges with courage and grace.

But "Unleashing Resilience" is not just a book about triumphing over adversity; it is also a celebration of the human spirit. Through heart-warming anecdotes, we will witness the power of compassion, kindness, and community in fuelling resilience. We will explore how the support of loved ones and the strength of human connection can help us weather life's storms.

Moreover, "Unleashing Resilience" is a call to action. As we journey through the chapters, you will be encouraged to take charge of your life and embrace resilience as a way of being. You will be challenged to step out of your comfort zone, face your fears, and seize opportunities for growth.

At the heart of this book is the belief that resilience is not a fixed trait; it is a skill that can be developed and nurtured. Through the power of storytelling, science, and practical exercises, "Unleashing Resilience" will equip you with the tools you need to thrive in the face of adversity.

So, are you ready to embark on this transformative journey? Are you ready to tap into the wellspring of resilience within you and unleash your full potential? If so, then join me as we dive into the extraordinary world of resilience, where ordinary individuals become heroes, and the human spirit shines brightest in the darkest of times.

Together, let's embrace resilience and create a life that defies the odds, a life that is filled with purpose, joy, and unwavering strength. Let's uncover the power of resilience and unleash the extraordinary within us all. Welcome to "Unleashing Resilience" - a journey that will change your life forever.

"
LIFE'S CHALLENGES DO NOT DEFINE US;
IT IS OUR RESILIENCE THAT SHAPES OUR DESTINY**"**

Introduction

Unleashing Resilience

In the vast tapestry of life, we all encounter countless threads of challenges, adversities, and unexpected turns. The symphony of our existence is orchestrated by moments of triumph and moments of defeat. Through this exquisite dance of fate, one thing remains constant: resilience. It is the invisible force that empowers us to rise above hardships and navigate the stormy seas of life.

Welcome to the remarkable journey of "Unleashing Resilience," where we embark on an exploration of human spirit and the extraordinary power it holds. In this chapter, we delve into the essence of resilience, understanding its profound impact, and uncovering the key to unlocking its full potential.

Section 1: Defining Resilience

1.1 The Resilience Spectrum

At the core of our being lies a spectrum of resilience, ranging from those who crumble under pressure to those who flourish in the face of adversity. We unravel the different facets of this spectrum and how it shapes our responses to life's challenges.

1.2 The Psychology of Resilience

What lies beneath the surface of resilience? We dive into the psychological aspects that influence our ability to bounce back, from mindset and emotional intelligence to coping mechanisms and learned behaviors.

1.3 The Science of Resilience

Resilience is not merely a concept; it is a well-researched phenomenon. We explore the scientific studies and groundbreaking research that offer insights into the neurological, physiological, and biochemical aspects of resilience.

Section 2: The Resilient Mindset

2.1 Embracing Adversity

Adversity is not the enemy; it is the crucible in which resilience is forged. We discover how embracing challenges and reframing our perception of difficulties can transform our outlook on life.

2.2 The Power of Positive Thinking

The mind is a powerful tool, and positive thinking can be the beacon of hope during the darkest hours. Uncover the science behind the "positive psychology" movement and how it influences our resilience.

2.3 Cultivating a Growth Mindset

Fixed or growth mindset - which one defines you? We delve into the profound impact of cultivating a growth mindset on our ability to overcome obstacles and embrace continuous personal development.

Section 3: Building Resilience

3.1 Building Emotional Resilience

Emotions can either paralyze us or propel us forward. In this section, we learn how to build emotional resilience, allowing us to acknowledge, manage, and harness the power of our emotions.

3.2 The Resilient Body

Physical well-being is a cornerstone of resilience. We explore the connection between mind and body, and how taking care of our physical health strengthens our capacity to face life's challenges.

3.3 Nurturing Social Resilience

Human beings are social creatures, and our support systems play a pivotal role in our resilience. We explore the power of connections, empathy, and fostering meaningful relationships.

In this inaugural chapter, we have taken the first steps in our journey of Unleashing Resilience. We have defined resilience, explored its psychological underpinnings, and discovered the importance of cultivating a resilient mindset. We have delved into the science behind resilience and how it manifests in our lives.

As we continue to delve deeper into the world of resilience, let us remember that we possess an inherent strength to rise above life's challenges. Together, we will unlock the secrets to Unleashing Resilience and uncover the limitless potential that lies within each of us.

"
WITHIN EVERY SETBACK LIES THE SEED OF
AN EVEN GREATER COMEBACK."

Embracing the Power Within

In the realm of resilience, the power to overcome adversity lies not in external circumstances, but within ourselves. Embracing the power within is the key to unleashing the full potential of resilience and propelling ourselves forward, no matter the challenges that come our way.

The Inner Source of Strength

When life throws us into the depths of despair, it is easy to seek solace in external factors. However, true resilience stems from recognizing that our greatest strength resides within. In this section, we explore the concept of inner resilience and how tapping into this source can transform our lives.

The Foundation of Self-Awareness

To embrace the power within, we must first embark on a journey of self-awareness. Understanding our emotions, triggers, and belief systems empowers us to confront challenges with clarity and poise. We delve into the practices of mindfulness and self-reflection as gateways to unlocking our inner strength.

The Power of Self-Belief

Our beliefs shape our reality, and self-belief is the cornerstone of resilience. Discover how cultivating unwavering faith in our abilities can turn the tides in our favor. We explore the concept of self-efficacy and the profound impact it has on our capacity to navigate life's obstacles.

The Art of Positive Affirmations

Words hold immense power; they can either elevate us or drag us down. In this section, we delve into the art of positive affirmations and how they serve as transformative tools to boost our resilience.

Rewriting Our Inner Narrative

The stories we tell ourselves about our capabilities significantly influence our response to challenges. We explore the practice of rewriting our inner narrative, replacing self-doubt with empowering affirmations. Through this process, we strengthen our resilience and transform our outlook on life.

The Science of Self-Talk

Affirmations are not just wishful thinking; they are grounded in science. We delve into the psychology of self-talk, understanding how positive affirmations rewire our neural pathways and create a mindset primed for resilience.

Harnessing the Power of Visualization

The mind is a canvas, and visualization is the paintbrush that allows us to create our destiny. In this section, we explore the transformative practice of harnessing the power of visualization to bolster our resilience.

Creating Mental Blueprints

Visualization is a powerful tool that enables us to create mental blueprints of our desired outcomes. We delve into the process of envisioning success, visualizing the steps to overcome challenges, and channeling our energy towards positive change.

From Imagination to Reality

The bridge between imagination and reality lies in focused action. We uncover the link between visualization and achievement, as well as the role it plays in maintaining unwavering determination during adversity.

Cultivating Emotional Intelligence

Emotions are the colours that paint the canvas of our experiences. Cultivating emotional intelligence is the key to embracing the power of our emotions and leveraging them as catalysts for resilience.

Emotional Awareness

Resilience is not about suppressing emotions, but rather understanding and embracing them. We explore the importance of emotional awareness and the role it plays in our ability to adapt and bounce back from setbacks.

Emotional Regulation

To embrace the power within, we must learn to regulate our emotions effectively. We delve into the practices of emotional regulation, discovering how to transform negative emotions into constructive fuel for growth.

Empathy and Resilience

Building resilience is not a solitary endeavor; it requires the support of others. Empathy fosters connections and strengthens our social support system, creating a network of resilience that sustains us during challenging times.

We have explored the profound significance of embracing the power within. The journey of self-awareness, the art of positive affirmations, and the transformative practice of visualization have empowered us to tap into our innate resilience.

“
WITHIN EVERY STORM LIES THE STRENGTH
TO WEATHER IT.„

1 The Resilience Mindset

In the unpredictable tapestry of life, the resilient mindset serves as the loom that weaves together the threads of strength, courage, and adaptability. It is the foundation upon which resilience is built, and the lens through which we view the world and its challenges. In this chapter, we embark on a journey to understand the resilient mindset and how it empowers us to navigate life's twists and turns with grace.

1.1 Embracing Change as an Opportunity

Change is the only constant in life, and the resilient mindset recognizes it as an opportunity rather than a threat. We explore the power of reframing our perspectives on change, viewing it as a catalyst for growth and transformation. Embracing change opens doors to new possibilities, fostering a mindset that welcomes challenges as stepping stones towards our aspirations.

1.2 The Strength of Optimism

Optimism is the beacon that guides us through the darkest of storms. In this section, we uncover the strength of optimism as a core component of the resilient mindset. We delve into the science behind positive thinking, understanding how an optimistic outlook enhances our problem-solving abilities and bolsters our resilience in the face of adversity.

1.3 Cultivating a Growth Mindset

The resilient mind is rooted in the belief that abilities and intelligence can be developed through dedication and hard work. Cultivating a growth mindset empowers us to view failures as stepping stones to success, embrace challenges as opportunities to learn, and persistently strive for excellence. We explore the principles of a growth mindset and its transformative impact on our resilience.

1.4 The Art of Adaptability

Adaptability is the cornerstone of resilience, enabling us to bend with the winds of change without breaking. In this section, we uncover the art of adaptability and its profound role in our ability to navigate through life's uncertainties. We learn to let go of rigidity, embrace the unfamiliar, and embrace change as an integral part of our journey.

1.5 Nurturing Self-Compassion

In our pursuit of resilience, we often forget the importance of self-compassion. This section sheds light on the significance of treating ourselves with kindness and understanding during difficult times. Nurturing self-compassion allows us to bounce back from setbacks, learn from failures, and build a deeper sense of self-worth.

1.6 The Power of Positivity

Positivity is not just a fleeting emotion; it is a way of life for the resilient mind. We explore the transformative power of positivity and its ripple effects on our mental and emotional well-being. By cultivating positivity, we create a reservoir of strength that sustains us during life's trials.

1.7 Harnessing Resilient Thinking

Resilient thinking is the fuel that propels us forward, even in the face of daunting challenges. This section delves into the mechanics of resilient thinking, such as reframing setbacks as opportunities for growth, seeking solutions rather than dwelling on problems, and nurturing a sense of purpose in every endeavour.

1.8 Building Resilience through Mindfulness

Mindfulness is the anchor that keeps us grounded in the present moment, allowing us to respond to adversity with clarity and composure. We explore the practice of mindfulness and its role in building resilience by cultivating awareness, reducing stress, and fostering a deeper connection with ourselves and the world around us.

As we go through our exploration of the resilient mindset, we recognize that resilience is not an elusive trait possessed by a select few; rather, it is a mindset that can be cultivated and strengthened through intentional practices. Embracing change, fostering optimism, cultivating a growth mindset, embracing adaptability, nurturing self-compassion, harnessing the power of positivity, and practicing mindfulness are the building blocks of resilience.

Building Mental Toughness

In the crucible of life's challenges, mental toughness emerges as the steel that fortifies our spirit and empowers us to endure, thrive, and achieve our aspirations. It is the ability to remain steadfast in the face of adversity, to embrace discomfort as an opportunity for growth, and to rise above setbacks with unwavering resolve. In this section, we embark on a journey to understand the essence of mental toughness and how we can cultivate this indomitable trait within ourselves.

The Foundations of Mental Toughness

At the core of mental toughness lie resilience, grit, and a growth mindset. We explore how these foundational elements synergistically strengthen our mental fortitude. Resilience enables us to bounce back from adversity, while grit fuels our perseverance and relentless pursuit of our goals. A growth mindset, as we discovered in the previous chapter, empowers us to view challenges as opportunities for growth and learning.

Harnessing the Power of Self-Belief

Belief in oneself is the seed from which mental toughness blossoms. We delve into the significance of self-belief and how it propels us to surpass our perceived limitations. Through inspiring stories and scientific insights, we uncover the transformative impact of self-belief on our ability to face challenges head-on and unlock our full potential.

Embracing Discomfort as a Catalyst for Growth

The path to mental toughness is not paved with ease; it is marked by discomfort and uncertainty. In this section, we explore the art of embracing discomfort as a catalyst for growth. By venturing beyond our comfort zones, we build resilience, develop new skills, and unlock reservoirs of untapped potential within ourselves.

The Power of Positive Self-Talk

Our inner dialogue shapes our reality, and positive self-talk lays the foundation for mental toughness. We uncover the power of affirmations, visualization, and constructive self-talk in building mental resilience. By cultivating a kind and encouraging inner voice, we bolster our confidence and create a wellspring of strength to draw upon during challenging times.

Developing Emotional Intelligence

Emotional intelligence is the art of understanding and managing our emotions and those of others. We explore how emotional intelligence enhances mental toughness by enabling us to navigate through difficult emotions, build meaningful relationships, and foster a deeper sense of empathy and compassion towards ourselves and others.

Cultivating a Strong Support System

The journey towards mental toughness is not one that we embark upon alone. Our support systems—family, friends, mentors—form the bedrock of our resilience. In this section, we delve into the importance of cultivating a strong support system, seeking guidance and encouragement from those who uplift and inspire us on our path to mental toughness.

Building Resilience through Mind-Body Connection

The mind and body are intricately connected, and in this section, we explore how physical well-being contributes to mental toughness. Regular exercise, adequate sleep, and mindful practices play a vital role in reducing stress, improving cognitive function, and bolstering our capacity to face challenges with equanimity.

The Art of Perseverance

Perseverance is the beacon that guides us through the darkest of tunnels. We uncover the art of perseverance—staying the course despite obstacles, failures, and setbacks. Drawing inspiration from the stories of remarkable individuals who transformed adversity into triumph, we learn to cultivate the unwavering determination that defines mental toughness.

Navigating Through Challenges

Life is a journey full of unexpected twists and turns. Challenges are an inevitable part of this expedition, and they often test the resilience of even the strongest individuals. The ability to navigate through these challenges with grace and determination is a defining trait of a resilient person.

In this section, we will explore the various strategies and mindsets that can help you successfully navigate through life's challenges and emerge stronger and wiser on the other side.

1. Embracing Change

One of the first steps in navigating through challenges is to embrace change. Change is a constant in life, and resistance to it can lead to stress and unhappiness. Resilient individuals understand that change is a natural part of growth and development. They learn to adapt and even welcome new circumstances, viewing them as opportunities for learning and personal growth.

2. Developing a Growth Mindset

Having a growth mindset is crucial in navigating challenges. A growth mindset is the belief that abilities and intelligence can be developed through dedication and hard work. People with a growth mindset see setbacks as opportunities to learn and improve, rather than as signs of failure. By cultivating a growth mindset, you can approach challenges with a positive and proactive attitude, which can significantly impact your ability to overcome them.

3. Cultivating Self-Compassion

In times of difficulty, it is essential to practice self-compassion. Self-compassion involves treating yourself with kindness and understanding, just as you would a close friend. Instead of being overly critical or judgmental, resilient individuals acknowledge their struggles with compassion and empathy. This self-compassion not only fosters emotional well-being but also provides a solid foundation for overcoming challenges with resilience.

4. Building a Support System

Navigating challenges becomes more manageable when you have a strong support system. Surrounding yourself with supportive and caring individuals can provide emotional and practical assistance during difficult times. Whether it's family, friends, or mentors, a support system can offer encouragement, advice, and a listening ear when you need it the most.

5. Setting Realistic Goals

Setting realistic goals is another crucial aspect of navigating through challenges. Resilient individuals break down daunting tasks into smaller, achievable goals. This approach not only provides a sense of accomplishment but also allows for a step-by-step approach to overcoming challenges. By focusing on attainable objectives, you can maintain motivation and momentum throughout your journey.

6. Developing Problem-Solving Skills

Problem-solving is a valuable skill that helps you navigate through challenges effectively. Resilient individuals approach problems with a solution-oriented mindset. They analyze the situation, identify potential solutions, and take decisive action to address the issue. Developing strong problem-solving skills empowers you to tackle obstacles with confidence and resourcefulness.

7. Cultivating Emotional Intelligence

Emotional intelligence plays a vital role in navigating challenges and maintaining mental well-being. Understanding and managing your emotions can help you cope with stress and adversity more effectively. Resilient individuals are in tune with their feelings and can regulate them in healthy ways. This emotional self-awareness allows them to stay composed and focused during challenging times.

8. Practicing Mindfulness and Stress Reduction

Practicing mindfulness and stress reduction techniques can significantly enhance your ability to navigate through challenges. Mindfulness involves being present in the moment and observing your thoughts and feelings without judgment. It can help you stay grounded and focused, even amidst difficult circumstances. Stress reduction techniques such as deep breathing, meditation, or engaging in hobbies can help you manage stress and maintain a clear perspective during challenging times.

9. Cultivating Resilient Thinking

Resilient thinking involves reframing negative thoughts and adopting a positive outlook. Resilient individuals practice cognitive flexibility, which allows them to view challenges from different perspectives. By challenging negative beliefs and focusing on positive possibilities, you can build resilience and maintain an optimistic attitude, even in the face of adversity.

10. Learning from Setbacks

Setbacks are an inherent part of any journey, and navigating through challenges often involves learning from these setbacks. Resilient individuals view setbacks as valuable learning experiences. Instead of dwelling on failures, they reflect on what went wrong, what lessons they can take away, and how they can improve in the future. This growth-oriented approach to setbacks fuels personal development and strengthens resilience.

Navigating through challenges is not a linear process but rather a dynamic journey of self-discovery and growth. By embracing change, developing a growth mindset, cultivating self-compassion, building a support system, setting realistic goals, developing problem-solving skills, cultivating emotional intelligence, practicing mindfulness, and adopting resilient thinking, you can build the resilience needed to overcome life's challenges with strength and grace. Remember that resilience is not about being invincible, but about bouncing back and thriving despite adversity. As you embark on this journey of unleashing your resilience, you will discover the tremendous power within you to face life's challenges with courage and resilience.

The Power of Positive Thinking

"Your attitude, not your aptitude, will determine your altitude."

- Zig Ziglar

Positive thinking is a powerful tool that can significantly impact your resilience and overall well-being. It involves maintaining an optimistic outlook and focusing on the possibilities rather than the limitations. When faced with challenges, resilient individuals harness the power of positive thinking to overcome obstacles and move forward with confidence. In this section, we will explore the science and psychology behind positive thinking and how you can cultivate a positive mindset to bolster your resilience.

1. The Science of Positive Thinking

Numerous studies have demonstrated the profound effects of positive thinking on mental and physical health. When you engage in positive thinking, your brain releases chemicals like endorphins and dopamine, which are responsible for feelings of happiness and pleasure. These chemicals not only improve your mood but also boost your immune system and reduce stress levels.

Moreover, positive thinking has been linked to improved cognitive function, creativity, and problem-solving abilities. When you approach challenges with a positive mindset, you are more likely to think outside the box and come up with innovative solutions.

2. The Power of Positive Affirmations

Positive affirmations are powerful statements that reinforce positive beliefs and attitudes. By repeating affirmations daily, you can rewire your brain to focus on the positive aspects of life and counteract negative self-talk. Resilient individuals use positive affirmations to build self-confidence and inner strength, especially during challenging times.

For example, instead of telling yourself, "I can't do this," replace it with "I am capable, and I can handle whatever comes my way." By consistently affirming positive beliefs, you empower yourself to face challenges with courage and optimism.

3. Cultivating Gratitude

Gratitude is a fundamental aspect of positive thinking and resilience. When you cultivate gratitude, you shift your focus from what you lack to what you have. Resilient individuals practice gratitude daily, acknowledging and appreciating the blessings and opportunities in their lives.

Keeping a gratitude journal, where you write down things you are grateful for each day, is an effective way to cultivate gratitude. This practice not only fosters a positive mindset but also helps you find joy in the little things and stay resilient during difficult times.

4. The Optimism Bias

The optimism bias is a cognitive bias that causes individuals to overestimate the likelihood of positive outcomes and underestimate the likelihood of negative ones. While this bias may seem unrealistic, it plays a crucial role in building resilience.

Resilient individuals tend to exhibit the optimism bias, believing that things will work out for the best in the end. This positive outlook fuels their motivation to persevere through challenges and find opportunities in setbacks.

5. Overcoming Negative Thinking Patterns

Negative thinking patterns can hinder resilience and perpetuate a cycle of self-doubt and pessimism. It is essential to recognize and challenge these patterns to cultivate a positive mindset.

One common negative thinking pattern is catastrophizing, where you imagine the worst possible outcomes in any situation. To overcome this pattern, practice reframing negative thoughts into more balanced and realistic ones.

For instance, if you catch yourself thinking, "This situation is a disaster, and I'll never recover from it," reframe it as, "This situation is challenging, but I have overcome difficulties in the past, and I can do it again."

6. The Power of Visualization

Visualization is a technique used by many resilient individuals to achieve their goals and overcome obstacles. By vividly imagining yourself successfully navigating through challenges and achieving your desired outcomes, you create a mental blueprint for success.

When you visualize success, your brain begins to perceive it as more attainable, motivating you to take action and persevere. Incorporate visualization into your daily routine, and you will find yourself approaching challenges with newfound confidence and determination.

7. Resilient Role Models

Resilient role models can inspire and reinforce your positive thinking. Learning about individuals who have faced adversity and triumphed can give you the courage to persevere through your own challenges.

Read biographies or watch documentaries of people who have displayed remarkable resilience, and draw lessons from their experiences.

By seeing how others have overcome seemingly insurmountable obstacles, you will gain valuable insights and strength to navigate your journey with optimism.

The power of positive thinking lies in its ability to shape your perception of challenges and influence your responses to them. By harnessing the science of positive thinking, embracing positive affirmations, cultivating gratitude, recognizing the optimism bias, overcoming negative thinking patterns, utilizing visualization, and drawing inspiration from resilient role models, you can unleash the transformative power of positivity in your life.

Positive thinking empowers you to embrace challenges with courage, see setbacks as opportunities for growth, and maintain a resilient mindset in the face of adversity. As you cultivate the art of positive thinking, you will discover the extraordinary strength and resilience that lies within you, propelling you towards a life of fulfilment, growth, and unwavering optimism.

"
STRENGTH DOES NOT COME FROM PHYSICAL CAPACITY.
IT COMES FROM AN INDOMITABLE WILL. "

– MAHATMA GANDHI

2 Cultivating Inner Strength

"The bamboo that bends is stronger than the oak that resists."

In the journey of life, we encounter countless challenges that test our resilience. As we navigate through the trials and tribulations, we come to realize that true strength lies not in stubborn resistance, but in the ability to adapt and flow like the bamboo in the wind. In this chapter, we delve deeper into the art of cultivating inner strength – a profound quality that enables us to endure, evolve, and thrive amidst the storms of life.

Embracing Vulnerability and Authenticity

In a world that often values invulnerability and the appearance of strength, embracing vulnerability might seem counterintuitive. However, it is in acknowledging and accepting our vulnerabilities that we discover our true strength. Vulnerability is not a sign of weakness; rather, it is a reflection of our humanity. When we open ourselves up to vulnerability, we create authentic connections with others, foster empathy, and pave the way for personal growth. Like a seedling breaking through the soil to reach for the sun, our vulnerabilities allow us to grow and bloom.

Life is filled with uncertainties and challenges, and the fear of vulnerability can hold us back from fully experiencing the richness of life. By embracing our vulnerabilities, we break free from the shackles of fear and open ourselves to new possibilities. It is through vulnerability that we tap into our deepest emotions, find the courage to heal, and discover our true resilience.

Harnessing the Power of Mindfulness

In the midst of chaos and turbulence, finding inner strength can seem like an impossible task. But within each of us lies a sanctuary of calm – the present moment. Mindfulness, the practice of being fully present and aware of our thoughts, feelings, and sensations, is a powerful tool that helps us navigate the ups and downs of life with grace and resilience.

In a fast-paced world, we often find ourselves lost in the whirlwind of worries and regrets about the past or anxieties about the future. Mindfulness anchors us in the here and now, enabling us to let go of the past and the future, and find peace in the present. Through mindfulness, we become attuned to our inner selves, gain clarity about our emotions, and develop a deep sense of self-awareness.

With mindfulness, we learn to respond to challenges rather than react impulsively. This subtle shift in our approach empowers us to make conscious choices and navigate through difficult situations with wisdom and resilience. By cultivating mindfulness, we create a space for inner strength to flourish and illuminate our path, even in the darkest of times.

The Art of Self-Compassion

Amidst the trials and tribulations, we often tend to be our harshest critic. We berate ourselves for our mistakes, dwell on our shortcomings, and hold ourselves to unrealistic standards. However, true inner strength is born not from self-criticism but from self-compassion.

Self-compassion is the practice of treating ourselves with the same kindness, understanding, and compassion that we would offer to a dear friend. It involves acknowledging our imperfections and embracing our humanness with warmth and acceptance. When we cultivate self-compassion, we create a nurturing environment within ourselves, allowing for growth and healing to take place.

Instead of allowing self-criticism to weaken our spirits, self-compassion bolsters our resilience. It helps us bounce back from setbacks, learn from our experiences, and find the strength to carry on. Self-compassion is not a form of self-indulgence; rather, it is a profound act of self-care that nurtures our well-being and empowers us to face life's challenges with grace and determination.

By embracing vulnerability, harnessing the power of mindfulness, and practicing self-compassion, we cultivate the seeds of inner strength within us. As we journey through the chapters of life, we discover that true resilience is not just about weathering the storms but about blossoming into our fullest selves – like the bamboo that bends gracefully, yet stands tall and strong in the face of adversity.

In the next chapter, we explore the concept of emotional intelligence and how it intertwines with resilience, empowering us to navigate the intricate landscapes of human emotions and relationships.

Emotional Resilience

Navigating the Turbulent Seas of Emotions

In the tempestuous sea of life, emotions ebb and flow like waves, sometimes gentle and calming, and at other times turbulent and overwhelming. Emotional resilience is the art of riding these emotional waves with grace and fortitude, navigating through the storms of feelings while staying grounded in our inner strength. It empowers us to face life's challenges without being swept away by the tumultuous tides of emotions.

Emotions are an inherent part of the human experience, and they can range from joy and love to sadness, anger, and fear. It is important to remember that experiencing negative emotions does not make us weak; rather, it is a testament to our humanity. Emotional resilience is not about suppressing or denying emotions; instead, it is about acknowledging and processing them in a healthy and constructive manner.

1. Understanding the Emotion Ocean

Emotional resilience begins with understanding our emotional landscape. Like explorers of our own minds and hearts, we learn to identify and label our emotions, recognizing them as passing clouds in the vast sky of consciousness. By gaining insight into our emotional responses, we become better equipped to navigate through challenging situations without being engulfed by the intensity of our feelings.

One powerful tool for understanding emotions is mindfulness. As we practice mindfulness, we become observers of our emotions, creating a space between the emotion and our response. This space allows us to choose how we wish to react, rather than being driven solely by the tide of emotions. With this newfound awareness, we can cultivate emotional intelligence and respond to situations with greater clarity and balance.

2. Resilience in the Face of Adversity

Life is replete with adversities – the loss of a loved one, career setbacks, relationship challenges, and unexpected events that shake the very foundation of our existence. Emotional resilience is the lighthouse that guides us through these tumultuous waters, providing a steady beacon of hope and courage.

Resilience does not mean that we are impervious to pain or that we never experience distress. On the contrary, resilience is about acknowledging the pain and distress and finding ways to adapt and grow through the experience. It is about recognizing that even in the darkest moments, there is a glimmer of light, and with time, that light will grow stronger.

During times of adversity, it is essential to lean on our support systems – family, friends, or professional help – to weather the storms. Seeking help is not a sign of weakness; it is an act of self-compassion and strength. By allowing ourselves to be vulnerable and asking for support, we build deeper connections with others, strengthening our emotional resilience.

3. Cultivating Emotional Regulation

Emotional regulation is the rudder that steers us through the ever-changing currents of emotions. It involves being aware of our emotions, understanding their triggers, and finding healthy ways to manage and express them. When faced with intense emotions, emotional regulation empowers us to respond rather than react impulsively.

One powerful technique for emotional regulation is deep breathing. By taking slow, deep breaths, we activate the parasympathetic nervous system, which calms the body's stress response. This simple practice allows us to centre ourselves and regain emotional balance in the midst of challenging situations.

Another key aspect of emotional regulation is developing a sense of self-compassion. Instead of judging ourselves for experiencing certain emotions, we offer ourselves understanding and kindness. Just as we would comfort a friend in distress, we extend the same care to ourselves, fostering a nurturing and supportive inner environment.

4. Building Resilient Coping Mechanisms

Resilience is not a trait we are born with; rather, it is a skill that we can cultivate and strengthen over time. Building resilient coping mechanisms is akin to constructing a sturdy sail that helps us navigate through life's unpredictable waters.

One powerful coping mechanism is reframing – the practice of viewing challenges from a different perspective. By reframing a difficult situation, we can find hidden opportunities for growth and learning. This shift in perception empowers us to approach challenges with a sense of curiosity and optimism.

Another resilient coping mechanism is seeking meaning and purpose in life's experiences. When faced with adversity, finding meaning can offer solace and motivation to move forward. By aligning our actions with our values and purpose, we derive strength and resilience from a deeper sense of meaning.

5. The Role of Emotional Support

Emotional support is like a lifeboat that keeps us afloat during the storms of life. Connecting with others who understand and validate our emotions creates a sense of belonging and safety. This support network provides a space to express ourselves authentically and openly without fear of judgment.

During challenging times, seeking professional help from therapists or counsellors can provide invaluable guidance and tools to enhance emotional resilience. These professionals can assist us in developing healthy coping strategies and in navigating through difficult emotions.

In conclusion, emotional resilience is a journey of self-discovery and growth, allowing us to embrace the full spectrum of our emotions and

Overcoming Adversity

Life is not always smooth sailing. Each of us encounters adversities, challenges, and setbacks at some point in our journey. It is during these testing times that our resilience is put to the ultimate test. Overcoming adversity requires a unique blend of inner strength, perseverance, and the ability to adapt to change.

1. Embracing Change as an Opportunity

Adversity often comes in the form of unexpected changes - a job loss, a relationship ending, a health crisis, or a financial setback. These events can shake us to our core and leave us feeling lost and disoriented. However, the key to overcoming adversity lies in how we perceive and respond to change.

Resilient individuals view change as an opportunity for growth and transformation. Instead of resisting the inevitable, they embrace change with an open mind and heart. They understand that every challenge presents an opportunity to learn, evolve, and become stronger.

2. Developing a Growth Mindset

At the heart of overcoming adversity is the development of a growth mindset. A growth mindset is the belief that our abilities and intelligence can be developed through dedication and hard work. Individuals with a growth mindset see failures and setbacks as stepping stones to success, rather than roadblocks.

When faced with adversity, those with a growth mindset ask themselves, "What can I learn from this experience? How can I grow and improve?" By reframing challenges as opportunities for learning and development, they maintain a positive outlook and a sense of hope even in the face of adversity.

3. Resilience in the Face of Setbacks

Adversity often brings with it setbacks and obstacles. Resilience is the ability to bounce back from these setbacks and continue moving forward despite the difficulties. Resilient individuals do not let failure define them; instead, they view it as a temporary setback and use it as a stepping stone to future success.

To build resilience, it is crucial to focus on self-compassion and self-care. Resilient individuals prioritize their well-being, both physical and emotional, during challenging times. They seek support from friends, family, or professionals and do not hesitate to ask for help when needed.

4. The Power of Adaptability

Adversity often requires us to adapt to new circumstances and situations. The ability to be flexible and adapt to change is a hallmark of resilience. Those who can embrace change and adapt quickly are better equipped to navigate the turbulent waters of adversity.

Adaptable individuals view change as an opportunity to learn and grow. They let go of rigid expectations and embrace uncertainty with a sense of curiosity and openness. This flexibility allows them to find innovative solutions and navigate through challenging situations with grace and resilience.

5. Finding Meaning and Purpose

During times of adversity, it is essential to find meaning and purpose in our experiences. Finding purpose gives us the motivation to persevere and overcome obstacles. It provides us with a sense of direction and focus, even in the darkest of times.

Those who can find meaning in their adversity often emerge from challenging situations with a greater sense of clarity and purpose. They may discover new passions, embark on a journey of self-discovery, or find a deeper connection to their values and beliefs.

6. Cultivating Supportive Relationships

No one can overcome adversity alone. Supportive relationships play a significant role in helping us navigate through difficult times. Surrounding ourselves with compassionate and understanding individuals can provide the emotional support and encouragement needed to face adversity head-on.

Resilient individuals build and maintain strong support systems. They lean on their friends, family, or community when they need a listening ear or a helping hand. These relationships provide a sense of belonging and security, fostering resilience and the courage to face challenges.

Overcoming adversity is an inherent part of the human experience. Life's challenges test our resilience and inner strength. By embracing change as an opportunity, developing a growth mindset, building resilience, and cultivating supportive relationships, we can navigate through adversity with courage and determination.

Adversity has the power to transform us and reveal the depths of our inner resilience. It challenges us to tap into our inner reserves of strength and adaptability. Through the power of resilience, we can emerge from adversity with newfound wisdom, growth, and a deeper appreciation for the journey of life.

Harnessing the Strength of Vulnerability

Vulnerability is often seen as a weakness, a state of being exposed and defenceless. However, when harnessed consciously and courageously, vulnerability can become a wellspring of inner strength and resilience. In this section, we explore the transformative power of vulnerability and how embracing our vulnerabilities can lead to greater emotional fortitude.

1. Redefining Vulnerability

Contrary to popular belief, vulnerability is not a flaw but a fundamental aspect of our human experience. It is the essence of authenticity, the courage to show up as our imperfect selves, and the willingness to be seen, even when it feels uncomfortable.

When we suppress vulnerability, we create walls that disconnect us from our emotions and from others. Embracing vulnerability, on the other hand, allows us to forge deeper connections and build meaningful relationships. It enables us to lean into discomfort, take risks, and grow beyond our self-imposed limitations.

2. Cultivating Emotional Resilience through Vulnerability

Emotional resilience is not about shielding ourselves from difficult emotions but about developing the capacity to navigate through them with grace and courage. Embracing vulnerability is a gateway to emotional resilience, as it encourages us to confront our emotions honestly and authentically.

When we acknowledge and express our vulnerabilities, we release the emotional weight that holds us back. This process fosters emotional agility, allowing us to move through challenging emotions with greater ease and self-compassion.

3. Vulnerability as a Catalyst for Growth

In vulnerability lies the potential for tremendous growth. It is through facing our vulnerabilities that we discover our inner strength and learn to embrace imperfections as opportunities for learning and growth.

Sharing our vulnerabilities with others creates a space for empathy and understanding. It allows us to connect on a deeper level and recognize that we are not alone in our struggles. In this shared vulnerability, we find strength as a collective, supporting each other through life's trials and triumphs.

4. The Power of Vulnerability in Relationships

Vulnerability is the foundation of authentic and intimate relationships. When we open ourselves up to vulnerability with our loved ones, we create a safe space for emotional intimacy and connection.

Sharing vulnerabilities with a partner or friend can deepen the bond, fostering trust and mutual support. It encourages open communication, allowing us to express our needs and emotions honestly. In return, our vulnerability inspires others to be open and honest with us, creating a reciprocal and nurturing dynamic.

5. Vulnerability as a Path to Self-Discovery

Embracing vulnerability requires us to confront our fears and insecurities. In doing so, we embark on a journey of self-discovery, uncovering aspects of ourselves that we may have hidden away.

Through vulnerability, we gain insight into our desires, values, and passions. It encourages us to confront limiting beliefs and break free from self-imposed barriers. Embracing vulnerability as a path to self-discovery empowers us to lead more authentic and fulfilling lives.

6. Overcoming Fear of Judgment

The fear of judgment often holds us back from embracing vulnerability. We worry about how others will perceive us, fearing rejection or criticism. However, acknowledging that vulnerability is an inherent part of being human can help us release the grip of judgment.

When we fully accept ourselves, vulnerabilities and all, we become less reliant on external validation. We learn to cultivate self-compassion and recognize that our worthiness is not determined by the opinions of others.

7. The Vulnerable Leader

In leadership, vulnerability can be a powerful tool for building trust and fostering a positive organizational culture. Leaders who embrace vulnerability demonstrate authenticity and humility, creating an environment where employees feel safe to express their ideas and concerns.

A vulnerable leader acknowledges their mistakes and takes responsibility for their actions. This transparency fosters trust and respect among team members, leading to increased collaboration and innovation.

8. Vulnerability and Creativity

Vulnerability is intimately connected with creativity. When we allow ourselves to be vulnerable, we tap into the depths of our emotions and experiences. This well of vulnerability becomes a source of inspiration for creative expression.

Many artists, writers, and musicians draw from their vulnerabilities to create art that resonates with others. Through their vulnerability, they touch the hearts of their audiences and create profound connections.

9. Setting Boundaries with Vulnerability

While vulnerability can be empowering, it is essential to set healthy boundaries to protect ourselves from exploitation or harm. Not every situation or person warrants our vulnerability, and discernment is key.

By establishing clear boundaries, we can open up authentically to those we trust while safeguarding ourselves from potential emotional harm. Setting boundaries with vulnerability empowers us to share our truths without compromising our emotional well-being.

10. Cultivating Self-Compassion in Vulnerable Moments

In moments of vulnerability, self-compassion becomes our most potent ally. Instead of criticizing ourselves for feeling exposed or uncertain, we offer ourselves kindness and understanding.

Practicing self-compassion helps us view our vulnerabilities with greater acceptance and non-judgment. It reminds us that it is okay to be imperfect and that vulnerability is a testament to our humanity.

11. Vulnerability and Resilience in the Workplace

In the corporate world, vulnerability is often associated with weakness. However, progressive organizations recognize the power of vulnerability in fostering a culture of innovation and resilience.

Leaders who model vulnerability create an environment where employees feel empowered to take risks and embrace failure as a stepping stone to success. This culture of psychological safety fuels creativity and adaptability, making the organization more resilient to change.

12. The Hero's Journey of Vulnerability

Joseph Campbell's "Hero's Journey" is a powerful framework that parallels the path of vulnerability. The hero faces trials and challenges, embracing their vulnerabilities along the way. Through this journey, they emerge transformed, armed with newfound wisdom and strength.

Embracing vulnerability is our hero's journey, where we confront our fears and emerge stronger on the other side. As we navigate through vulnerability, we write our own narrative of resilience and growth.

13. Vulnerability and Radical Acceptance

Radical acceptance is the practice of fully embracing our reality, no matter how challenging it may be. It involves accepting our vulnerabilities and limitations without judgment, freeing us from the burden of self-criticism. By practicing radical acceptance, we become more resilient in the face of adversity. Instead of resisting or denying our vulnerabilities, we integrate them into our identity, accepting ourselves wholeheartedly.

14. Empathy and Vulnerability

Empathy is the ability to understand and share the feelings of another person. When we embrace vulnerability, we become more attuned to the emotions of others, deepening our capacity for empathy.

Empathy fosters connection and support, creating a network of compassion that bolsters resilience in the community. As we embrace vulnerability and cultivate empathy, we build bridges of understanding that span differences and unite us as human beings.

In conclusion, vulnerability is not a weakness to be avoided but a source of inner strength and resilience. Embracing vulnerability allows us to connect authentically with ourselves and others, paving the way for personal growth and transformation. By harnessing the power of vulnerability, we navigate through the trials and tribulations of life with greater courage, compassion, and resilience.

Case Study

Embracing Vulnerability for Personal Growth

Meet Sarah, a 32-year-old marketing executive who seemed to have it all together. She had a successful career, a loving partner, and a supportive circle of friends. However, beneath the surface, Sarah was struggling with feelings of inadequacy and self-doubt. The pressure to maintain a facade of perfection in her professional and personal life was taking a toll on her emotional well-being.

Sarah's journey toward embracing vulnerability began when she attended a workshop on emotional resilience and inner strength. The speaker talked about the transformative power of vulnerability and how it could lead to greater emotional fortitude. Intrigued by the concept, Sarah decided to explore vulnerability further.

For Sarah, vulnerability had always been associated with weakness. She believed that showing her true emotions and struggles would make her appear less competent and in control. However, through the workshop, she learned that vulnerability was not a flaw but a fundamental aspect of the human experience.

As Sarah started to embrace vulnerability, she noticed a shift in her emotional resilience. Instead of suppressing her emotions, she allowed herself to feel them fully and express them authentically. This newfound emotional agility allowed her to navigate through challenging emotions with greater ease and self-compassion.

Sarah's journey of vulnerability became a catalyst for personal growth. As she shared her vulnerabilities with her partner and close friends, she found a deeper sense of connection and support. The act of being seen and understood for her authentic self-empowered her to break free from the fear of judgment and rejection.

Sarah's vulnerability also transformed her relationships. By opening up to her partner about her fears and insecurities, she created a safe space for emotional intimacy and honesty. This newfound vulnerability fostered trust and mutual support, strengthening the foundation of their relationship.

Embracing vulnerability became a journey of self-discovery for Sarah. As she confronted her fears and insecurities, she gained insight into her desires, values, and passions. This self-exploration empowered her to shed limiting beliefs and embrace her authentic self.

Initially, Sarah feared that being vulnerable would lead to judgment and criticism from others. However, as she embraced vulnerability more fully, she realized that the opinions of others did not define her worthiness. Her ability to accept herself, vulnerabilities and all, allowed her to let go of the need for external validation.

In her professional life, Sarah found that vulnerability could also be a powerful tool for leadership. By embracing vulnerability, she created an environment where her team felt safe to express their ideas and concerns. Her transparency and willingness to admit mistakes fostered trust and respect among her team members, leading to increased collaboration and innovation.

Through her journey of embracing vulnerability, Sarah discovered a wellspring of inner strength and resilience. By allowing herself to be seen and heard in her authentic state, she cultivated deeper connections in both her personal and professional life. Sarah's transformation serves as a real-life case study of how harnessing vulnerability can lead to personal growth, stronger relationships, and increased emotional resilience.

This case study illustrates the transformative power of vulnerability in cultivating inner strength and resilience. Sarah's journey serves as an inspiring example of how embracing vulnerability can lead to personal growth and stronger connections with others. Through her courage to face her fears and insecurities, Sarah was able to find a sense of authenticity and empowerment in her life. Her story demonstrates the extraordinary potential that lies within each of us to harness vulnerability as a path to greater resilience and fulfilment.

3 Thriving in Relationships

In the story of life, relationships are the intricate threads that weave our journey together. Whether it's the unbreakable bond with family, the camaraderie of friendships, or the romantic connections that make our hearts flutter, relationships are the cornerstones of our existence. They have the power to uplift us to soaring heights or leave us broken and scarred. In this chapter, we embark on a journey to understand how resilience plays a pivotal role in fostering thriving relationships and creating a harmonious tapestry of love and support.

The Resilient Connection

At the heart of every flourishing relationship lies a resilient connection that weathers the storms of life. Building and maintaining this connection is a delicate dance that requires vulnerability, trust, and adaptability. It's about understanding that every relationship will face challenges, but it's how we respond to these challenges that shapes the course of the connection.

True resilience in relationships begins with self-awareness. Knowing ourselves and understanding our needs, fears, and insecurities allows us to show up authentically in our interactions with others. Embracing vulnerability is not a sign of weakness but a testament to our strength, as it opens the door to deep emotional intimacy.

It is also crucial to acknowledge that relationships require active effort and continuous communication. Just as a garden needs tending to thrive, relationships need care, attention, and nurturing. Life's unpredictable nature can bring unexpected twists and turns, but a resilient connection serves as an anchor that keeps us grounded.

Weathering Storms Together

Adversity is an inevitable part of life, and relationships are not exempt from its grasp. The strength of a relationship is often tested during these challenging times. It's during these storms that resilience becomes the guiding light that helps us navigate through the darkness.

Resilience in relationships isn't about avoiding conflicts or pretending everything is perfect. Rather, it's about-facing adversity together as a team. It's about being each other's rock when the world feels uncertain and providing unwavering support. In the face of adversity, resilient relationships become a safe haven where vulnerability is embraced, and emotions are met with empathy and understanding.

However, building resilience in relationships doesn't happen overnight. It requires patience, compassion, and a willingness to grow together. Just as a tree's roots dig deeper into the soil during storms, weathering challenges in relationships strengthens the bond between individuals.

Embracing Change and Growth

As we journey through life, change is a constant companion. Whether it's personal growth, shifting priorities, or unforeseen circumstances, change can either challenge or fortify relationships. Resilience in relationships means embracing change as an opportunity for growth rather than fearing it as a threat.

A resilient relationship is flexible and adaptable, capable of weathering the transformations that life brings. It's about supporting each other's aspirations and celebrating individual growth while fostering a shared vision for the future.

Communication is the lifeblood of resilient relationships. It allows us to navigate the ebb and flow of change, understand each other's evolving needs, and ensure that the connection remains strong despite the winds of change.

In the realm of relationships, resilience is the key that unlocks the door to enduring connections filled with love, trust, and support. Nurturing a resilient connection begins with understanding ourselves and showing up authentically. It means embracing vulnerability and opening our hearts to the beauty of human connection.

Resilience allows us to weather the storms that life throws our way, knowing that we have a steadfast partner by our side. It is a force that empowers us to grow, adapt, and thrive in the face of adversity.

let us embark on this journey to cultivate thriving relationships, for in doing so, we create a shades of love, strength, and resilience that withstands the tests of time.

Resilience in Love and Loss

Love and loss are two sides of the same coin, intertwined in the tapestry of human relationships. The profound experiences of love and the deep sorrow of loss test the limits of our emotional strength. In this section, we will explore how resilience plays a vital role in navigating the intricate web of emotions that arise from love and loss.

Love, the purest of emotions, has the power to lift us to heights of ecstasy and connection. It nurtures our souls, ignites our passions, and fills our hearts with boundless joy. Love bestows upon us the courage to take risks, to be vulnerable, and to trust. It is a force that binds two souls, making them stronger together than they could ever be apart.

Yet, with love, comes the potential for loss. The pain of losing someone we hold dear can shatter our world, leaving us feeling broken and vulnerable. It is in these moments of heartache that our resilience is truly put to the test.

Resilience in love and loss is not about avoiding pain or suppressing emotions. It is about acknowledging the depth of our feelings, embracing vulnerability, and finding the strength to navigate through the storms of grief. It is about honouring the memory of those we have lost while also allowing ourselves to open our hearts to new possibilities.

One of the greatest challenges of resilience in love and loss is learning to let go. When we lose someone, we love, it is natural to cling to their memory, to hold on tightly to the past. However, holding on too tightly can prevent us from moving forward and embracing new opportunities for love and connection.

Resilience teaches us to find the balance between cherishing the past and living in the present. It is about finding the strength to carry the memories of our loved ones in our hearts while also embracing the beauty of the present moment.

In the face of loss, resilience allows us to transform grief into growth. It gives us the courage to face our pain, to confront our fears, and to emerge from the darkness stronger and wiser. Resilience teaches us to see loss not as an end, but as a new beginning – a chance to redefine ourselves and our relationships.

Throughout history, there have been countless examples of individuals who have demonstrated remarkable resilience in the face of love and loss. The story of Queen Victoria, who mourned the loss of her beloved husband, Prince Albert, for the rest of her life but also found the strength to carry on her royal duties and responsibilities, is a testament to the power of resilience.

Similarly, the life of poet Maya Angelou, who endured a traumatic childhood and faced numerous personal struggles, is an inspiring example of how resilience can transform pain into purpose. Despite the challenges she faced, Angelou's indomitable spirit and resilience allowed her to rise above her circumstances and become a beacon of hope and inspiration for millions.

In our own lives, we may have experienced love and loss in various forms – the end of a romantic relationship, the loss of a dear friend, or the passing of a beloved family member. Each of these experiences tests our emotional resilience and challenges us to find strength in the midst of pain.

Practicing resilience in love and loss is not a one-time event but an ongoing journey. It requires self-compassion, patience, and a willingness to embrace the ebb and flow of emotions. It is about acknowledging that healing is not linear, and there will be moments of sadness even amidst joy.

Building resilience in love and loss also involves reaching out for support from others. It is in our connections with loved ones and our communities that we find comfort and solace during difficult times. Sharing our feelings with others and allowing ourselves to be vulnerable is an essential part of the healing process.

In conclusion, resilience in love and loss is a profound testament to the strength of the human spirit. It is the ability to find hope in the darkest moments, to transform pain into growth, and to honour the past while embracing the present. By cultivating resilience, we can navigate the complexities of love and loss with grace and courage, knowing that within us lies the capacity to endure and thrive.

Building Supportive Networks

Resilience in the face of life's challenges is not a solitary journey. It is built upon the foundation of supportive networks that surround us. In this section, we will delve into the importance of building and nurturing these networks to foster our resilience and well-being.

Human beings are social creatures, and our connections with others play a significant role in shaping our experiences and responses to adversity. Supportive networks provide us with a sense of belonging, validation, and empathy, which are crucial for maintaining emotional balance during challenging times.

1. The Power of Connection

At the heart of building supportive networks is the power of connection. These connections can take many forms – from close friendships and family bonds to professional networks and community affiliations. Each connection contributes to our overall sense of social support, offering a safety net that catches us when we stumble and propels us forward when we need encouragement.

2. Nurturing Authentic Relationships

Building supportive networks starts with nurturing authentic relationships. Authenticity fosters trust and openness, creating an environment where individuals feel safe to share their vulnerabilities and seek help without judgment. Authentic relationships are characterized by empathy, active listening, and a genuine desire to support one another.

3. Identifying Sources of Support

In times of adversity, it is essential to identify the sources of support in our lives. These sources can come from various areas, such as friends, family members, colleagues, mentors, or support groups. Being aware of our support systems allows us to reach out when needed and leverage the strength and wisdom of those around us.

4. Cultivating Resilient Communities

Supportive networks extend beyond individual relationships to encompass resilient communities. Resilient communities are characterized by a collective sense of purpose, shared values, and a commitment to supporting each other through challenges. These communities foster a sense of belonging and offer a wider network of support during difficult times.

5. The Role of Mentors

Mentors play a vital role in our journey towards resilience. A mentor is someone who guides and empowers us to navigate obstacles, offering insights from their own experiences and wisdom. Mentorship can come from various sources, such as senior colleagues, teachers, or community leaders, and serves as a valuable resource for personal and professional growth.

6. Balancing Reciprocity

Supportive networks thrive on reciprocity, where individuals give and receive support in equal measure. Striking a balance between giving and receiving allows for a sustainable network of support, where everyone benefits from the strength of collective resilience.

7. Building Online Supportive Networks

In the digital age, online communities and social media platforms provide opportunities to connect with like-minded individuals worldwide. Building online supportive networks can be especially beneficial for individuals facing unique challenges or seeking specialized support. However, it is essential to approach online interactions mindfully and verify the credibility of sources.

8. Facing Stigma and Seeking Support

In some cases, seeking support may be hindered by stigma or cultural barriers. Breaking through these barriers requires courage and vulnerability, but it can lead to profound personal growth and the discovery of supportive resources within our communities.

Case Study: The Power of Peer Support

Emily, a high-achieving student, was faced with overwhelming stress and anxiety as she prepared for her final exams. Feeling isolated and unable to cope, Emily's academic performance began to suffer. Recognizing the signs of distress, her teacher recommended she join a peer support group at school.

Initially hesitant, Emily decided to give it a try. In the support group, she found a safe space to share her struggles and fears with fellow students facing similar challenges. The group provided an empathetic and non-judgmental environment where everyone could offer their insights and coping strategies.

Through the support group, Emily not only gained practical tips for managing exam stress but also discovered a sense of camaraderie and validation. The peer support bolstered her confidence and helped her navigate through the difficulties she faced. Over time, Emily's grades improved, and she emerged from the experience with newfound resilience and a deeper appreciation for the power of supportive networks.

Building supportive networks is a transformative journey that enriches our lives and enhances our resilience. These networks serve as lifelines during turbulent times, offering understanding, encouragement, and a sense of belonging. By cultivating authentic relationships, embracing mentorship, and nurturing resilient communities, we can harness the collective strength of our networks to navigate the ups and downs of life with greater fortitude and grace.

Communication and Conflict Resolution

Effective communication is the cornerstone of healthy relationships and plays a pivotal role in building resilience. In this section, we will explore the power of communication in enhancing our ability to navigate conflicts and challenges with grace and understanding.

1. The Art of Active Listening

At the heart of effective communication is active listening. When we actively listen to others, we validate their experiences and emotions, creating a safe space for open dialogue. Active listening involves being fully present, giving our undivided attention, and seeking to understand rather than simply respond.

2. Expressing Vulnerability

Vulnerability is a fundamental aspect of effective communication. When we share our feelings and concerns with others, we foster deeper connections and create opportunities for empathy and support. Expressing vulnerability requires courage, but it is a powerful tool for building trust and resilience in relationships.

3. Empathy and Understanding

Empathy is the ability to understand and share the feelings of another person. Cultivating empathy allows us to see the world through the eyes of others and respond with compassion and understanding. When conflicts arise, approaching them with empathy can de-escalate tensions and lead to productive resolutions.

4. Nonviolent Communication

Nonviolent communication is a powerful communication style that focuses on expressing needs, feelings, and requests without blaming or criticizing others. By using nonviolent communication techniques, we can navigate conflicts in a constructive and respectful manner, fostering mutual understanding and cooperation.

5. Managing Emotions

Effective communication involves managing our emotions skillfully. During conflicts, emotions can run high, making it challenging to communicate rationally. Learning to recognize and regulate our emotions allows us to engage in productive discussions and find mutually beneficial solutions.

6. Conflict Resolution Strategies

Conflict is a natural part of human interaction, and learning to resolve conflicts constructively is essential for building resilience. Conflict resolution strategies involve active problem-solving, compromise, and a willingness to find common ground. By approaching conflicts with a collaborative mindset, we can turn challenges into opportunities for growth.

7. Effective Feedback and Criticism

Providing and receiving feedback is an integral part of communication. Constructive feedback helps us learn and improve, while criticism, when delivered in a respectful manner, can offer valuable insights. Learning to give and receive feedback with grace and openness fosters a culture of continuous improvement and resilience.

8. Cultivating Emotional Intelligence

Emotional intelligence is the ability to recognize, understand, and manage our emotions and those of others. Cultivating emotional intelligence enhances our communication skills and enables us to navigate complex social dynamics with empathy and insight.

9. Communicating Across Cultures

In a diverse and interconnected world, communicating across cultures is becoming increasingly important. Respectful and sensitive cross-cultural communication fosters understanding and inclusivity, bridging gaps and promoting harmonious relationships.

10. Digital Communication and Resilience

With the advent of digital communication, we must be mindful of how technology impacts our relationships and resilience. Nurturing authentic connections in the digital realm and using technology responsibly can enhance, rather than diminish, our resilience.

Case Study: Transforming Conflict through Communication

Sarah and Michael had been close friends since childhood, but as they entered adulthood, their lives took different paths. They began to drift apart, and misunderstandings started to brew between them. Instead of addressing these issues directly, they avoided confrontations and let resentment build.

One day, they found themselves in a heated argument over a minor disagreement. Frustration and hurt feelings came to the surface, and their friendship seemed to be on the brink of collapse. However, both Sarah and Michael recognized the value of their long-standing friendship and decided to address the underlying issues through open communication.

They scheduled a time to meet in person and allowed each other to express their feelings without interruption. They practiced active listening and tried to understand each other's perspectives. By expressing vulnerability and empathy, they could see how their own actions had contributed to the conflict.

Through constructive dialogue, Sarah and Michael were able to re-establish their friendship on a stronger foundation. They agreed to communicate more openly in the future and to address issues promptly instead of letting them fester. This experience taught them the importance of effective communication in preserving relationships and building resilience together.

Effective communication is an indispensable skill in fostering resilience and nurturing meaningful relationships. By practicing active listening, expressing vulnerability, and embracing empathy, we can navigate conflicts with grace and understanding. Through nonviolent communication and conflict resolution strategies, we can transform challenges into opportunities for growth. Cultivating emotional intelligence and communicating across cultures further enrich our connections with others and strengthen our ability to thrive in the face of adversity. As we harness the power of communication, we unlock the potential to build resilience within ourselves and within the world around us.

The Eternal Dance of Resilience

Once upon a time in a quaint little village nestled amidst rolling hills and lush greenery, there lived a young couple named Lily and Jack. They were deeply in love and had dreams of building a life together filled with happiness, love, and togetherness. Their love was like a blooming flower, vibrant and full of promise. They got married with the blessings of their families, and their future seemed bright with infinite possibilities.

Lily and Jack's love story began in their school days. They were inseparable, sharing dreams, aspirations, and supporting each other's passions. Their love flourished with every passing day, and their hearts intertwined as if destiny had woven their souls together.

One fateful day, tragedy struck the village as a devastating storm swept through, leaving destruction and heartache in its wake. Lily and Jack's home was not spared from the havoc, and they lost all their belongings. But what hurt them the most was the loss of their unborn child in the midst of the chaos. The storm left scars on their hearts that seemed impossible to heal.

The loss of their child brought immense grief and emotional turmoil to Lily and Jack. Each of them dealt with the pain differently, finding themselves adrift in a sea of sorrow. The weight of grief seemed too heavy to bear, and at times, they felt distant from each other, unable to bridge the chasm of sorrow that had grown between them.

In their darkest moments, Lily and Jack sought guidance from the wise elder of the village, Grandma Rose. She had seen many storms in her lifetime and knew the secret to weathering them. She advised them to seek support from their friends and family, to lean on each other, and to not be afraid to share their pain. Grandma Rose reminded them that strength was not about standing alone but in holding each other up when life's tempests raged.

As Lily and Jack opened up about their grief, they found solace in knowing that they were not alone in their suffering. Their friends and family offered a listening ear and a shoulder to cry on, providing much-needed empathy and understanding. This connection with their loved ones brought them comfort and strength, reminding them that love could be a balm to soothe the deepest wounds.

With Grandma Rose's guidance, Lily and Jack learned to embrace vulnerability and share their deepest fears and insecurities. They realized that it was okay to lean on each other for support and to express their vulnerabilities without judgment. This newfound openness deepened their emotional bond, and they found solace in the safe haven of each other's arms.

As the days turned into weeks and the weeks into months, Lily and Jack began to rebuild their lives with resilience and determination. They faced the challenges of rebuilding their home and their hearts with unwavering strength. Their love for each other served as a beacon of hope in the darkest times, guiding them through the stormy seas of grief and loss. Through their journey of resilience, Lily and Jack discovered that thriving in relationships meant embracing both love and loss. They learned that it was okay to feel joy amidst grief and to find moments of happiness in the midst of adversity. Their love became a source of strength, and together, they found the courage to face whatever life threw their way, hand in hand, united in their love and strength.

Lily and Jack's story is a profound reminder that the true essence of resilience lies not in avoiding the storms of life, but in dancing through them with love and unwavering support. They showed us that even in the darkest hours, the power of love and vulnerability can heal even the deepest wounds. Their journey serves as an eternal testament to the strength of the human spirit and the boundless capacity of love to withstand the trials of life. May their story inspire us all to embrace resilience, to thrive in the face of adversity, and to dance through life's storms with love in our hearts.

A MIND RESILIENT, LIKE STARS ALIGNED,
THROUGH LIFE'S TURBULENCE, IT'S REDEFINED.

4 The Resilient Mind

Navigating Life's Turbulence

In the vast expanse of life's journey, each soul encounters storms and tempests that test the very fabric of its existence. Such turbulent moments are inevitable and can leave us feeling helpless and overwhelmed. However, it is within the depths of these trials that the true power of the resilient mind emerges—a force that enables us to navigate the unpredictable waters with strength, grace, and unyielding determination.

The mind, the enigmatic centre of our being, holds the key to weathering life's storms. It is here, in the inner sanctuary of our thoughts, that resilience takes root. A resilient mind is not impervious to difficulties, but it possesses the remarkable ability to bounce back from adversity, to adapt and transform, and to find opportunity amidst chaos.

The journey towards cultivating a resilient mind is one of self-discovery and introspection. It requires us to embrace our vulnerabilities and acknowledge our limitations, for it is through this acceptance that we find the strength to rise again. The resilient mind understands that growth stems from challenges and that every obstacle encountered is an opportunity to learn and evolve.

To embark on the path of resilience, we must first understand the dynamics of our thoughts and emotions. Like the ebb and flow of the tides, emotions can be tumultuous, threatening to capsize our inner equilibrium. Yet, within this very turbulence, lies the power to harness the energy of emotions and channel it towards constructive ends.

Emotional intelligence becomes the guiding star, helping us navigate through the choppy waters of emotional turmoil. The ability to recognize and manage our feelings enables us to respond to life's challenges with clarity and wisdom. It is the anchor that keeps us steady amidst the storm, preventing us from being tossed about by the whims of circumstance.

In this chapter, we delve into the multifaceted nature of the resilient mind, exploring the power of emotional intelligence, mindfulness, and the practice of gratitude. We uncover the significance of self-compassion, empowering us to be gentle with ourselves in times of difficulty. Moreover, we embark on a journey of self-discovery, understanding the importance of aligning our core values with our actions, fostering inner congruence.

The art of cultivating a resilient mind is a symphony of practices that harmonize with one another, creating a rhythm that empowers us to navigate the turbulence of life with grace and dignity. Just as a skilled sailor learns to read the signs of the wind and waves, we too learn to read the currents of our emotions and thoughts, guiding us towards the shores of serenity.

Join me on this transformative journey, where we embrace the beauty of imperfection, dance with our emotions, and unleash the potential of our resilient minds. As we navigate life's turbulence, we learn to rise above the waves and set sail towards the horizon, for it is in the face of adversity that the true resilience of the human spirit shines brightest.

Grit and Growth Mindset

In the crucible of life, where challenges and obstacles abound, the twin pillars of grit and growth mindset emerge as guiding beacons, illuminating the path to resilience and personal growth. Grit, that indomitable spirit that keeps us moving forward in the face of adversity, and growth mindset, the belief in our capacity to learn and improve, form a formidable alliance that empowers us to overcome obstacles and achieve greatness.

Grit is the relentless perseverance to pursue long-term goals with unwavering passion and determination. It is the grit that enables us to endure setbacks, push through failures, and keep going when the road ahead seems steep and arduous. Grit is not merely resilience; it is the courage to confront challenges head-on, to embrace discomfort, and to thrive amidst uncertainty.

The concept of grit is eloquently captured in the words of Angela Duckworth, a pioneering psychologist who defined it as "passion and perseverance for long-term goals." It is the unyielding commitment to one's purpose and the unwavering resolve to stay the course, even when the tides of adversity threaten to engulf us.

Grit is not a trait bestowed upon a select few at birth, but rather a quality that can be cultivated and nurtured. It is forged through the crucible of experience, as we face life's challenges and learn from our successes and failures. Grit is not measured by how many times we fall, but by how many times we rise, and it is in the act of rising that we discover our true strength.

A growth mindset, on the other hand, is the belief that our abilities and intelligence can be developed through effort and perseverance. It is the understanding that our talents are not fixed but can be nurtured and expanded with dedication and hard work. The concept of growth mindset, popularized by the pioneering work of Carol Dweck, has revolutionized our understanding of human potential.

With a growth mindset, we view challenges as opportunities for learning and growth. We embrace the concept of "not yet," understanding that we may not have mastered a skill or achieved a goal yet, but with effort and persistence, we can continue to improve and progress. A growth mindset empowers us to see failure not as a reflection of our abilities, but as a stepping stone on the path to success.

In this chapter, we delve into the profound insights of grit and growth mindset, exploring how these powerful mindsets intertwine to fuel our resilience and foster our personal growth. We uncover the secrets of cultivating grit and nurturing a growth mindset, discovering practical strategies to overcome self-limiting beliefs and embrace the power of possibility.

We explore the stories of individuals who exemplify grit and growth mindset, from renowned athletes who triumphed against all odds to ordinary people who turned adversity into opportunity. Their tales inspire us to embrace the grit within and adopt a growth mindset that opens the door to limitless possibilities.

Moreover, we recognize the critical role of self-compassion in the pursuit of grit and growth. To cultivate grit and foster a growth mindset, we must be kind to ourselves, acknowledging our imperfections and embracing failure as a natural part of the journey. Self-compassion becomes the balm that heals the wounds of disappointment and enables us to rise stronger and wiser.

As we embark on the exploration of grit and growth mindset, we uncover the interplay of these mindsets in our daily lives. We learn to recognize the moments of challenge and adversity as invitations to cultivate grit and embrace growth. With each step forward, we unleash the power within us to forge ahead with courage, tenacity, and an unwavering belief in our ability to grow and evolve.

Grit and growth mindset become our steadfast companions, empowering us to thrive amidst life's uncertainties and emerge stronger and more resilient on the other side. As we journey through the terrain of grit and growth mindset, we discover that within us lies an unyielding wellspring of strength and possibility, waiting to be unleashed.

Bouncing Back from Setbacks

Life's journey is fraught with inevitable setbacks – moments when our best-laid plans unravel, when we stumble and fall. In these moments of despair and disappointment, the essence of resilience reveals itself – the ability to bounce back from setbacks with newfound strength and wisdom.

Setbacks are not signs of weakness; they are the universal threads that weave through the fabric of human experience. Each setback carries with it valuable lessons and insights that, when embraced, become catalysts for growth and transformation. It is in the aftermath of setbacks that the true test of resilience emerges – the capacity to rise from the ashes and forge ahead with renewed determination.

The art of bouncing back from setbacks lies not in avoiding failure or adversity but in embracing them as integral parts of the journey. In these moments, the power of resilience reveals its transformative force, allowing us to harness the energy of disappointment and channel it towards growth.

Embracing Resilience in the Face of Adversity

At the heart of bouncing back from setbacks is the recognition that setbacks are not defining moments; they are opportunities for reinvention. When we view adversity as a teacher rather than a tormentor, we unlock the door to resilience. It is through the crucible of challenges that we are shaped and refined, emerging stronger, wiser, and more compassionate.

Resilience, however, is not a one-size-fits-all formula; it is a deeply personal and individual journey. What works for one may not work for another. As we navigate the labyrinth of setbacks, we discover the unique combination of tools and strategies that resonate with our spirit and empower us to rise.

The Power of Mindset in Overcoming Setbacks

Our mindset becomes a formidable ally in the face of setbacks. Embracing a growth mindset, we recognize that setbacks are not permanent roadblocks but stepping stones towards success. We cultivate a positive outlook, acknowledging setbacks as temporary detours on the road to our dreams.

With a growth mindset, we shed the shackles of self-doubt and embrace the belief that our abilities are not fixed but can be honed and expanded. This shift in mindset liberates us from the fear of failure, allowing us to approach setbacks with a spirit of curiosity and resilience.

Resilience is not the absence of vulnerability, but the willingness to embrace vulnerability as a source of strength. We allow ourselves to feel the pain of setbacks without being consumed by it, recognizing that vulnerability is a gateway to emotional healing and growth.

Cultivating Inner Resilience

At the core of bouncing back from setbacks lies the cultivation of inner resilience – a wellspring of strength that emanates from within. Inner resilience is not a fleeting burst of courage but a deep-rooted sense of self-belief that sustains us through the darkest of times.

The practice of mindfulness and self-compassion becomes our refuge in moments of setback. We treat ourselves with kindness and understanding, acknowledging that setbacks are an inherent part of the human experience. In the embrace of self-compassion, we find solace and healing, enabling us to navigate the storm with grace and fortitude.

Embracing Change and Adaptability

Setbacks are often harbingers of change, calling us to adapt and evolve. Resilience lies not in clinging to the past but in embracing the winds of change with open arms. As we cultivate adaptability, we learn to navigate the ever-changing tides of life with flexibility and grace.

In the face of setbacks, we must shed the rigidity of our old selves and embrace the fluidity of growth. Resilience is the art of surrendering to change without losing our sense of self. In the dance of adaptability, we find the courage to relinquish the old and embrace the new with open hearts.

The Triumph of Perseverance

Setbacks test our endurance and perseverance, urging us to stay the course even when the journey seems insurmountable. It is in the act of perseverance that the seeds of resilience bear fruit. We draw strength from the knowledge that setbacks are not the end of the road but stepping stones towards our goals.

Perseverance is not a solitary endeavor; it thrives in the embrace of community and support. We lean on the shoulders of loved ones and kindred spirits, finding solace and encouragement in their unwavering presence. In the togetherness of perseverance, setbacks lose their power to crush our spirit.

Finding Meaning in Setbacks

At the heart of resilience lies the quest for meaning amidst setbacks. It is in the search for purpose that we transcend the pain of setbacks and discover the transformative potential of adversity. Setbacks become the crucible of growth, offering us the chance to realign our values and priorities.

In the quest for meaning, we discover that setbacks are not roadblocks but detours that lead us to uncharted territories. The meaning we find in setbacks becomes the compass that guides us on our journey, steering us towards a life of purpose and fulfillment.

As we navigate the terrain of setbacks, we emerge with a profound understanding – setbacks are not the end of the journey but the beginning of a new chapter. In the tapestry of life, setbacks are the threads that create intricate patterns of resilience, strength, and wisdom. Each setback becomes a testament to our ability to rise, to adapt, and to embrace the beauty of imperfection.

In the embrace of resilience, we learn to dance with life's turbulence, knowing that storms will come, but they too shall pass. We become the captains of our own ships, navigating the turbulent seas with courage and grace. And as we weather the storms, we emerge with a newfound appreciation for the journey itself – the highs and the lows, the triumphs and the setbacks, the joys and the sorrows.

The journey of resilience is not linear; it is a winding path with twists and turns. But in the midst of uncertainty, we find the strength to keep moving forward, one step at a time. We embrace the unknown with a sense of adventure, knowing that every step leads us closer to our true selves.

In the tapestry of life, resilience is the golden thread that weaves through every chapter, connecting our past, present, and future. It is the thread that binds us to our inner strength and to each other. It is the thread that holds us together when everything seems to be falling apart.

And so, we embark on this journey of resilience, knowing that we are not alone. We walk hand in hand with countless souls who have traversed this path before us, and with those who will walk it after us. We are part of a timeless lineage of resilience, and with each step we take, we add our own chapter to the story of human strength and courage.

So, let us embrace the challenges that come our way, for they are the stepping stones that lead us to greatness. Let us cultivate the resilience that lies within us, for it is the key that unlocks the doors of possibility. Let us navigate life's turbulence with grace and fortitude, for it is in the face of adversity that our true character is revealed.

As we journey through the chapters of life, let us remember that setbacks are not the end but the beginning of something new. They are the catalysts that propel us forward, the lessons that shape us, and the moments that define us.

And so, let us be brave in the face of adversity, for in doing so, we unleash the power of resilience within us. Let us stand tall amidst life's storms, for it is in the face of turbulence that we discover our true strength. Let us embrace the challenges and setbacks, for they are the threads that weave the tapestry of our lives.

This book is an exploration of resilience – a journey through the chapters of human strength, courage, and perseverance. It is a testament to the power that lies within each of us, waiting to be unleashed. So, let us embark on this journey together, and may we emerge on the other side, stronger, wiser, and more resilient than ever before.

As mentioned earlier in the words of an ancient proverb, "The bamboo that bends is stronger than the oak that resists." Let us be like the bamboo, bending with the winds of adversity and finding strength in our flexibility. For it is in the art of bending, of adapting, and of bouncing back that we truly unleash the power of resilience within us.

The Triumph of Resilience

A Story of Courage and Perseverance

In the small town of Hopeville, nestled amidst lush green mountains, lived a young boy named Alex. From a very early age, Alex faced numerous challenges, as his family struggled to make ends meet. Despite the hardships, Alex always had a positive outlook on life. He believed that no matter how difficult the circumstances, he had the power to shape his destiny.

One day, tragedy struck when a devastating earthquake hit Hopeville, leaving destruction and despair in its wake. Alex's family lost their home, and they were forced to live in a makeshift shelter. The earthquake shattered the lives of many in the town, but it also brought out the resilience and strength of the community.

Amidst the chaos, Alex witnessed people coming together to support one another. They pooled their resources, offered shelter to those in need, and provided comfort to the grieving. This experience left a profound impact on Alex and ignited a fire within him to make a difference in the lives of others.

With determination and a growth mindset, Alex focused on his studies, despite the lack of resources. He knew education was his ticket to a better future. He walked several miles every day to reach the nearest school, and often studied late into the night by the dim light of a kerosene lamp.

His hard work paid off, and Alex's academic excellence caught the attention of a philanthropic organization that offered him a scholarship to pursue higher education. With this opportunity, Alex moved to the city, leaving behind his family and everything he knew.

In the city, Alex faced new challenges and setbacks. The fast-paced life and competitive environment were overwhelming. He struggled to fit in and often felt like an outsider. Despite his brilliance, he faced rejection from job interviews due to his humble background.

Feeling discouraged, Alex questioned his resilience and doubted his abilities. But deep inside, he knew he couldn't give up. He sought guidance from mentors and therapists to help him navigate the emotional turbulence he was experiencing.

Through counselling, Alex learned the power of self-compassion and reframing his setbacks as opportunities for growth. He embraced failure as a stepping stone to success and understood that setbacks were a natural part of the journey towards greatness.

With newfound resilience and determination, Alex kept pushing forward. He attended networking events, improved his communication skills, and sought out job opportunities that aligned with his passion for social impact.

As Alex continued on his journey, he realized that embracing vulnerability was a source of great strength. He opened up about his struggles and shared his story with others. To his surprise, he found that his vulnerability resonated with people. It inspired them to share their own stories and struggles, creating a sense of connection and support.

Alex's willingness to be vulnerable opened doors for him in unexpected ways. He was offered a position at a non-profit organization that worked with underprivileged communities. Here, he found a sense of purpose and fulfilment that he had been seeking all along.

In his role, Alex worked tirelessly to uplift the lives of those in need. He used his own experiences to empathize with others and provide them with the support and guidance they needed to overcome their own challenges. Through his work, he became a beacon of hope for countless individuals who had faced adversity.

The story of Alex is a testament to the power of resilience and the strength of the human spirit. It is a reminder that no matter how turbulent life may be, we have the capacity to bounce back from setbacks, to grow and evolve, and to harness the strength of vulnerability.

Through grit and a growth mindset, Alex transformed his life and the lives of others. His journey from a small town to the city, from adversity to triumph, serves as an inspiration to all who face challenges in their own lives.

The chapters of Alex's life were not always easy, but he navigated through the turbulence with courage, determination, and a resilient mind. His story shows us that with the right mindset and support, we too can overcome life's adversities and unleash the power of resilience within us.

"RESILIENCE BLOOMS WHERE SELF-CARE IS NURTURED."

5 Self-Care and Resilience

In the fast-paced and demanding world we live in, it's all too easy to get caught up in the whirlwind of responsibilities, expectations, and challenges. As we strive to meet the demands of work, family, and social life, we often neglect the most important person in our lives - ourselves.

Self-care is not a luxury; it is a fundamental necessity for fostering resilience and well-being. It is about nourishing our minds, bodies, and spirits so that we can navigate life's turbulence with grace and strength. In this chapter of "Unleashing Resilience," we embark on a journey of self-discovery and empowerment, exploring the transformative power of self-care and its profound impact on our ability to bounce back from adversity.

The Power of Self-Compassion

At the core of self-care lies self-compassion - the gentle, non-judgmental acceptance of ourselves, especially in times of struggle or failure. It is about treating ourselves with the same kindness, understanding, and support that we would offer to a dear friend. When we cultivate self-compassion, we create a safe space within ourselves, free from self-criticism and self-doubt.

Research has shown that self-compassion is not only linked to greater emotional well-being but also to increased resilience. When faced with challenges or setbacks, individuals with a strong sense of self-compassion are better equipped to cope with stress and adversity. They are less likely to be overwhelmed by negative emotions and more likely to bounce back from difficult experiences.

In these pages, we delve into the science and psychology of self-compassion, understanding its role in building resilience and emotional well-being. Through practical exercises and reflections, we learn how to be more compassionate towards ourselves, fostering a nurturing and empowering inner dialogue that fuels our resilience.

The Practice of Mindfulness

In a world filled with distractions and constant stimuli, mindfulness offers a refuge of presence and awareness. By cultivating mindfulness, we learn to be fully present in the here and now, without judgment or attachment to the past or future. This practice opens the door to greater self-awareness, emotional regulation, and a deeper connection with ourselves and others.

Mindfulness has been shown to reduce stress, anxiety, and depression while enhancing emotional resilience. It helps us cultivate a sense of inner peace and balance, allowing us to respond to challenges with clarity and wisdom. Mindfulness also enables us to appreciate the beauty and richness of life, even in the midst of difficulties.

In this chapter, we explore the art of mindfulness and its profound impact on our ability to navigate life's challenges. Through mindfulness practices, such as meditation, breathwork, and mindful movement, we discover the power of living in the present moment and building a solid foundation for resilience.

The Rituals of Self-Care

Self-care is not a one-time event; it is an ongoing practice of nurturing and replenishing ourselves. In this section, we delve into the rituals of self-care - the small, intentional acts that add up to create a life of balance and well-being.

Self-care rituals can take many forms, from engaging in regular exercise and eating nourishing foods to spending time in nature and connecting with loved ones. These rituals are not only essential for maintaining physical health but also for nourishing our emotional and spiritual well-being.

Through self-care rituals, we learn to prioritize our needs and set boundaries to protect our time and energy. We discover the joy of slowing down, savouring the present moment, and engaging in activities that bring us joy and fulfilment.

In "Unleashing Resilience," we explore a variety of self-care practices and provide practical tips on how to incorporate them into our daily lives. By making self-care a priority, we empower ourselves to navigate life's challenges with resilience and grace.

As we delve into the chapters ahead, let us remember that self-care is not selfish; it is an act of self-preservation and self-love. When we take care of ourselves, we are better able to care for others and show up fully in our lives.

Through the power of self-compassion, mindfulness, and self-care, we embark on a transformative journey towards greater resilience and well-being. Let us embrace these practices with an open heart and a curious mind, knowing that by nurturing ourselves, we unlock the true potential of our inner strength and resilience.

Prioritizing Well-being

In our fast-paced and demanding world, it's easy to get caught up in the hustle and bustle of daily life, often neglecting our own well-being in the process. However, the foundation of resilience lies in prioritizing our physical, emotional, and mental health. In this section, we explore the importance of making well-being a top priority and the transformative impact it has on our ability to navigate life's challenges.

The Role of Well-being in Resilience

Well-being is not just a luxury or a bonus; it is the cornerstone of resilience. When we prioritize our well-being, we build a strong and resilient foundation that enables us to face adversity with courage and strength.

Physical well-being, which encompasses aspects such as nutrition, exercise, and sleep, directly influences our ability to handle stress and bounce back from setbacks. When we take care of our bodies, we increase our energy levels, improve our immune system, and enhance our overall health and vitality.

Emotional well-being is equally vital for resilience. Emotions are a natural part of the human experience, and acknowledging and processing them is crucial for maintaining emotional balance. When we cultivate emotional intelligence and self-awareness, we become better equipped to cope with difficult emotions and build healthier relationships with ourselves and others.

Mental well-being involves nurturing a positive and growth-oriented mindset. A resilient mind is open to learning, embraces challenges as opportunities for growth, and maintains a sense of optimism and hope, even in the face of adversity.

By prioritizing our well-being, we invest in our ability to handle stress, regulate our emotions, and maintain a positive outlook on life - essential ingredients for resilience.

The Pillars of Well-being

To prioritize well-being, we must address its various pillars, each playing a unique role in supporting our resilience. Let's explore these pillars and discover how to integrate them into our lives.

Physical Health

Physical health is the foundation of overall well-being. Regular exercise, a balanced diet, and sufficient sleep are essential for nurturing our bodies and minds. Engaging in physical activity not only improves our physical health but also boosts our mood and reduces stress.

Nutrition is another crucial aspect of physical well-being. Consuming a diet rich in whole foods, fruits, and vegetables provides us with the nutrients needed for optimal physical and mental function.

Adequate sleep is equally vital for resilience. Quality sleep allows our bodies and minds to recover, promoting cognitive function and emotional regulation.

Emotional Intelligence

Emotional intelligence is the ability to recognize, understand, and manage our emotions effectively. It involves cultivating self-awareness, empathy, and healthy coping mechanisms.

When we are emotionally intelligent, we can identify our feelings and express them in a constructive manner. This awareness enables us to address underlying issues and find appropriate solutions.

Empathy is the ability to understand and relate to the emotions of others. By developing empathy, we build stronger connections and support networks, essential for resilience.

Healthy coping mechanisms, such as mindfulness and journaling, allow us to process emotions in a healthy and productive way, reducing the impact of stress on our well-being.

Mindfulness and Mindset

Mindfulness is the practice of being fully present in the moment, without judgment or attachment. It enables us to let go of past regrets and future worries, allowing us to focus on the here and now.

Mindfulness enhances our self-awareness, enabling us to recognize negative thought patterns and replace them with more positive and empowering ones.

A growth-oriented mindset is the belief that challenges and failures are opportunities for learning and growth. Embracing this mindset allows us to view setbacks as stepping stones on our journey to resilience.

4. Work-Life Balance

Achieving a healthy work-life balance is crucial for well-being and resilience. Balancing our personal and professional lives allows us to recharge and avoid burnout.

Setting boundaries and prioritizing self-care activities, such as hobbies and spending time with loved ones, can help us maintain a healthy work-life balance.

Integrating Well-being into Daily Life

Prioritizing well-being requires intentional effort and a commitment to self-care. Here are some practical strategies for integrating well-being into our daily lives:

Create a Self-Care Routine: Develop a daily self-care routine that includes activities such as exercise, meditation, or spending time in nature.

Practice Mindfulness: Engage in mindfulness practices, such as meditation or deep breathing exercises, to stay grounded and present.

Set Boundaries: Establish clear boundaries between work and personal life to avoid burnout and foster a sense of balance.

Nourish Your Body: Make healthy food choices that nourish your body and provide the energy needed for resilience.

Cultivate Emotional Intelligence: Practice self-reflection and empathy to enhance emotional intelligence and improve your relationships.

Adopt a Growth Mindset: Embrace challenges as opportunities for growth and view failures as learning experiences.

By prioritizing well-being and integrating these practices into our daily lives, we can enhance our resilience and ability to navigate life's turbulence with grace and strength.

Case Study: A Journey of Well-being and Resilience

Let's take a look at the inspiring journey of Sarah, a 35-year-old marketing executive, to understand the transformative power of prioritizing well-being in building resilience.

Sarah's life was a whirlwind of constant demands and stress. Between her demanding job, family responsibilities, and social commitments, she often felt overwhelmed and emotionally drained. She realized that she was neglecting her own well-being in the pursuit of success and validation from others.

One day, after experiencing a particularly challenging setback at work, Sarah decided that it was time to prioritize her well-being and build resilience. She began by creating a self-care routine, which included waking up early to practice meditation and setting aside time each evening for journaling and reflection. These practices allowed her to start each day with a clear and focused mind and end each day with a sense of gratitude and purpose.

Sarah also recognized the importance of setting boundaries and managing her workload effectively. She learned to say no to extra commitments that did not align with her priorities and to delegate tasks when necessary. This newfound assertiveness not only reduced her stress levels but also earned her respect from her colleagues and superiors.

As Sarah continued her journey, she began to notice a shift in her emotional well-being. She became more in tune with her emotions and developed healthy coping mechanisms to deal with stress and setbacks. Rather than suppressing her feelings, she allowed herself to experience them fully, giving herself the space to process and learn from them.

Sarah also adopted a growth mindset, seeing every challenge as an opportunity for personal and professional growth. She no longer feared failure but embraced it as a natural part of the learning process. This mindset allowed her to take risks and pursue new opportunities with confidence.

With her newfound resilience and well-being, Sarah became a source of inspiration for her colleagues and friends. They noticed her positive outlook on life and admired her ability to bounce back from adversity with grace and determination.

Through her journey of well-being and resilience, Sarah not only transformed her own life but also positively impacted the lives of those around her. Her story serves as a powerful reminder of the importance of prioritizing well-being and nurturing resilience to thrive in the face of life's challenges.

In this chapter, we have explored the critical role of well-being in building resilience. By prioritizing our physical, emotional, and mental health, and adopting healthy practices and mindsets, we can cultivate the inner strength needed to navigate life's turbulence with grace and fortitude. In the following chapters, we will continue to delve deeper into the facets of resilience, uncovering the secrets to unleashing our full potential and living life to the fullest.

Mindfulness and Meditation

In today's fast-paced and constantly changing world, it's easy to get caught up in the chaos of life. Our minds are often filled with worries about the future or regrets about the past, leaving little room for being present in the moment. This lack of mindfulness can lead to increased stress, anxiety, and a sense of disconnection from ourselves and those around us. However, by cultivating mindfulness and incorporating meditation into our daily lives, we can enhance our self-care and build resilience to navigate life's challenges with greater ease and clarity.

The Art of Mindfulness

Mindfulness is the practice of being fully present and aware of our thoughts, feelings, bodily sensations, and the environment around us. It involves observing our experiences without judgment, accepting them as they are, and letting go of the need to control or change them. When we cultivate mindfulness, we become more attuned to the present moment and develop a deeper understanding of ourselves and our inner world.

One way to practice mindfulness is through mindfulness meditation. This involves sitting quietly and focusing our attention on our breath, sensations in the body, or a particular object or thought. When our minds wander, as they inevitably will, we gently bring our attention back to the present moment, without criticizing ourselves for getting distracted. Over time, this practice helps us develop a greater sense of calm, clarity, and emotional resilience.

The Benefits of Mindfulness

Research has shown that mindfulness offers numerous benefits for our well-being and resilience. Regular practice of mindfulness meditation has been found to reduce stress, anxiety, and symptoms of depression. It can also improve our ability to focus, make better decisions, and regulate our emotions.

One of the key aspects of mindfulness is its ability to help us become more aware of our thoughts and emotions without being consumed by them. This skill is particularly valuable in challenging situations, as it allows us to respond with greater clarity and compassion rather than reacting impulsively out of fear or anger.

Case Study: Mindfulness in the Midst of Chaos

Let's take a look at the story of David, a 42-year-old executive, to understand the power of mindfulness in building resilience.

David's job as a senior executive in a fast-paced tech company was highly demanding. He often found himself juggling multiple responsibilities, and the pressure to meet tight deadlines and deliver results was overwhelming. This constant stress was taking a toll on his physical and emotional well-being.

Feeling burnt out and on the verge of a breakdown, David decided to explore mindfulness as a means of finding inner peace and balance. He started attending mindfulness meditation classes and incorporating short meditation sessions into his daily routine.

As David continued his mindfulness practice, he began to notice subtle shifts in his outlook on life. He became more patient and less reactive in stressful situations, allowing him to approach challenges with a calmer and more rational mindset. He also developed a greater sense of empathy and understanding toward his colleagues, leading to improved communication and collaboration within the team.

David's mindfulness practice also helped him become more attuned to his own needs and boundaries. He learned to recognize the early signs of stress and fatigue, allowing him to take proactive steps to prevent burnout. He started prioritizing self-care activities, such as exercise and spending time with loved ones, which further contributed to his overall well-being.

Over time, David's resilience grew stronger, and he found that he was better equipped to handle the ups and downs of his high-pressure job. He became more adaptable and open to change, embracing challenges as opportunities for growth rather than obstacles to overcome.

David's journey is a testament to the transformative power of mindfulness in building resilience. By cultivating a mindful awareness of his thoughts and emotions, he was able to navigate the turbulence of his professional life with greater ease and grace.

The Practice of Meditation

Meditation is another powerful tool for building resilience and self-care. It involves intentionally focusing the mind and eliminating distractions to promote relaxation and mental clarity. Meditation practices can vary widely, ranging from focused attention on the breath or a specific thought to loving-kindness meditation, where we cultivate feelings of compassion and goodwill toward ourselves and others.

Regular meditation practice has been found to reduce stress and promote emotional well-being. It can also enhance our ability to regulate emotions and improve our overall mental health. Studies have shown that individuals who meditate regularly experience reduced levels of cortisol, the stress hormone, and increased activity in brain regions associated with positive emotions and resilience.

The Journey of Self-Discovery

In addition to its physiological benefits, meditation is a journey of self-discovery. As we sit in silence and turn our attention inward, we begin to uncover the layers of conditioning and beliefs that shape our thoughts and actions. Through this process of self-awareness, we gain insight into our patterns of behavior and can make conscious choices to cultivate positive habits and let go of destructive ones.

The Transformative Power of Self-Compassion

Self-compassion is an essential aspect of self-care and resilience. It involves treating ourselves with the same kindness and understanding that we would offer to a close friend. In moments of difficulty or failure, self-compassion allows us to acknowledge our imperfections without judgment and offer ourselves the support and encouragement we need to keep moving forward.

Research has shown that self-compassion is strongly linked to resilience and well-being. People who practice self-compassion are more likely to bounce back from setbacks, experience less anxiety and depression, and have a greater sense of life satisfaction.

Case Study: The Power of Self-Compassion

Meet Sarah, a 30-year-old marketing manager who was struggling with feelings of inadequacy and self-doubt. Whenever she faced a setback at work or received negative feedback, Sarah would be incredibly hard on herself, feeling like a failure and questioning her abilities.

Through therapy and self-reflection, Sarah discovered the concept of self-compassion and began to integrate it into her life. She learned to recognize the harsh inner critic that often dominated her thoughts and started replacing it with a kinder and more compassionate voice.

As Sarah practiced self-compassion, she noticed a profound shift in her mindset and emotional well-being. When faced with challenges, she approached herself with understanding and patience, recognizing that everyone makes mistakes and experiences setbacks. Instead of spiraling into self-criticism, Sarah chose to treat herself with the same care and support she would offer to a friend.

Over time, Sarah's self-compassion practice helped her build resilience and navigate life's turbulence with greater ease. She became more accepting of her imperfections and saw failure as an opportunity for growth and learning. This newfound sense of self-compassion not only improved her well-being but also positively impacted her relationships and performance at work.

The Importance of Self-Care

Self-care is a foundational aspect of resilience, providing us with the strength and energy to cope with life's challenges effectively. It involves making conscious choices to prioritize our physical, emotional, and mental well-being.

Self-care looks different for everyone, as it involves activities and practices that nurture and replenish our unique needs. It can include regular exercise, healthy eating, getting enough sleep, spending time in nature, engaging in hobbies, and taking time for relaxation and reflection.

Building Inner Strength

In this section, we delve deeper into the practices and strategies that can help us build inner strength and resilience. These are the pillars of self-care that support us in navigating life's turbulence with grace and fortitude.

The Power of Gratitude

Gratitude is a simple yet profound practice that has the power to shift our perspective and transform our lives. It involves consciously focusing on the positive aspects of our lives and appreciating the blessings, big and small, that we often take for granted.

Research has shown that cultivating gratitude can lead to increased happiness, improved relationships, and enhanced well-being. When we practice gratitude regularly, we train our minds to notice the good even in challenging circumstances, fostering a sense of optimism and hope.

Case Study: Transformative Gratitude

Consider the story of Maya, a 25-year-old artist, who was struggling with feelings of discontent and dissatisfaction. Despite achieving success in her career, Maya often felt unfulfilled and unsatisfied with her life.

Through therapy, Maya was introduced to the practice of gratitude. She started keeping a gratitude journal, where she would write down three things she was grateful for each day. Initially, Maya found it challenging to come up with things to write about, but as she persisted, she began to notice a shift in her perspective.

Maya started to appreciate the little joys and blessings in her life, such as a beautiful sunrise, a kind gesture from a friend, or a moment of creative inspiration. As she focused on these positive aspects of her life, Maya's sense of fulfillment and contentment grew.

The practice of gratitude also helped Maya navigate difficult times with greater resilience. During a period of artistic blockage, instead of succumbing to self-doubt, she turned to her gratitude practice and reminded herself of her past achievements and the joy she found in creating art.

Over time, Maya's gratitude practice became a source of strength and inspiration in her life. It not only improved her emotional well-being but also deepened her connection with others and enriched her creative process.

Cultivating Optimism

Optimism is the belief that positive outcomes are possible, even in the face of adversity. It's the ability to see challenges as temporary and surmountable, and to have confidence in our ability to overcome them.

Optimism is not about denying or ignoring the difficulties we face but rather approaching them with a hopeful and solution-oriented mindset. It's a way of reframing setbacks and failures as opportunities for growth and learning.

Research has shown that optimism is strongly linked to resilience. People who cultivate optimism are better equipped to cope with stress, experience less anxiety and depression, and have a greater sense of well-being.

Nurturing Resilience in Others

In this section, we explore the significance of nurturing resilience in others, whether as parents, educators, leaders, or friends. Building a supportive and empowering environment for those around us can enhance their ability to navigate life's challenges with strength and courage.

The Power of Empathy

Empathy is the ability to understand and share the feelings of others. It involves being present with someone in their pain or struggle, offering a listening ear, and validating their emotions.

When we practice empathy, we create a safe and supportive space for others to express themselves authentically. This fosters a sense of connection and belonging, which is essential for building resilience.

Case Study: Empathy in Action

Meet Peter, a teacher known for his incredible ability to connect with his students. One day, Peter noticed that one of his students, Lily, seemed withdrawn and distant. Instead of ignoring her behaviour or reprimanding her, Peter decided to have a private conversation with her.

During their talk, Lily opened up about her parents' recent divorce and how it was affecting her emotionally. Peter listened attentively, offering a compassionate and understanding presence. He reassured Lily that it was okay to feel upset and encouraged her to share her thoughts and feelings with him whenever she needed to.

Over the following weeks, Peter continued to check in with Lily, providing her with a sense of stability and support during a challenging time. He also connected her with a school counselor and other resources to help her cope with her emotions.

Through Peter's empathy and support, Lily gradually began to find her footing again. She started participating in class activities and interacting with her peers more confidently. Peter's genuine care and understanding had a profound impact on Lily's resilience, helping her navigate the difficult period of her parents' divorce with greater strength and optimism.

Promoting a Growth Mindset

A growth mindset is the belief that our abilities and intelligence can be developed through effort, learning, and perseverance. It's the understanding that challenges and failures are opportunities for growth and that we can always improve and learn from our experiences.

As parents, educators, or leaders, nurturing a growth mindset in others is essential for fostering resilience. When we encourage others to embrace challenges, take risks, and view setbacks as learning opportunities, we empower them to develop a sense of resilience and confidence in their abilities.

Finding Purpose and Resilience

In this section, we explore the profound connection between finding purpose and building resilience. Having a sense of purpose provides us with the drive and determination to overcome obstacles and pursue our goals

Balancing Work and Life

In today's fast-paced and demanding world, finding a balance between work and life is a constant challenge. As we strive to excel in our careers and achieve our goals, it's essential not to overlook the importance of nurturing our personal lives and overall well-being.

The Modern Dilemma

In this era of connectivity and remote work, the boundaries between work and personal life have become increasingly blurred. Many individuals find themselves constantly tethered to their devices, responding to work emails and messages at all hours, and sacrificing their personal time and well-being in the process.

The consequences of this imbalance can be significant—burnout, decreased productivity, strained relationships, and compromised mental and physical health. Hence, achieving work-life balance is crucial for our overall happiness and resilience.

Defining Work-Life Balance

Work-life balance is not about achieving a perfect fifty-fifty split between work and personal life. It's about finding a harmony that allows us to meet our professional commitments while also making time for activities and relationships that bring us joy and fulfilment.

This balance will look different for each individual, as it depends on personal priorities, values, and life circumstances. What's important is that we consciously assess and adjust our commitments to ensure that we don't neglect any critical aspect of our lives.

Setting Boundaries

One of the keys to achieving work-life balance is setting clear boundaries between work and personal life. This involves defining specific work hours, creating dedicated spaces for work and relaxation, and resisting the temptation to check work-related communication during personal time.

By setting boundaries, we signal to ourselves and others that our personal time is valuable and deserves our full attention. It also helps us recharge and replenish our energy, making us more focused and productive when we are at work.

Time Management

Effective time management is another essential aspect of achieving work-life balance. By prioritizing tasks, setting realistic goals, and learning to delegate, we can optimize our productivity and create more space for personal activities and relationships.

One helpful approach to time management is the "Eisenhower Matrix," which categorizes tasks into four quadrants based on their urgency and importance. This method allows us to focus on tasks that align with our long-term goals while avoiding the trap of constantly dealing with urgent but non-essential matters.

The Role of Flexibility

In today's dynamic work environment, flexibility can be a game-changer in achieving work-life balance. Employers who embrace flexible work arrangements, such as remote work and flexible hours, enable their employees to better manage their personal responsibilities and achieve a healthier work-life integration.

For employees, embracing flexibility means learning to adapt to different circumstances and making the most of available resources. It also involves open communication with employers and colleagues to ensure that work commitments are met while also taking care of personal needs.

Mindfulness in Work and Life

Mindfulness is a powerful tool in achieving work-life balance. By practicing mindfulness, we cultivate self-awareness and present-moment awareness, allowing us to fully engage in both work and personal activities without being overwhelmed by distractions or stress.

Mindfulness practices such as meditation, deep breathing, and mindful movement can help us become more attuned to our physical and emotional needs. This, in turn, enables us to make conscious choices that support our well-being and work-life balance.

Nurturing Personal Relationships

Investing time and effort in building and nurturing personal relationships is a vital component of work-life balance. Meaningful connections with family, friends, and loved ones provide a sense of support, belonging, and happiness that can buffer us against the stresses of work.

However, maintaining personal relationships requires intentional effort and presence. It means being fully present during quality time with loved ones and making time for shared activities and meaningful conversations.

The Rewards of Work-Life Balance

When we achieve work-life balance, the rewards are profound. We experience reduced stress and burnout, improved physical and mental health, enhanced productivity and creativity, and more profound connections with others.

Moreover, a balanced life allows us to bring our best selves to both our personal and professional endeavors. We become more focused, compassionate, and resilient, better equipped to navigate life's challenges with grace and strength.

In this chapter, we explored the importance of achieving work-life balance in today's fast-paced world. By setting boundaries, managing our time effectively, embracing flexibility, and practicing mindfulness, we can create a harmonious integration of work and personal life.

Work-life balance is not a one-time achievement but an ongoing practice that requires constant reflection and adjustment. By prioritizing our well-being and nurturing personal relationships, we can lead more fulfilling and resilient lives.

Unveiling Resilience

The Journey to Work-Life Harmony in the Vibrant Streets of Jaipur

In the vibrant city of Jaipur, India, lived a young woman named Riya. Jaipur, with its rich culture and bustling streets, provided a colorful backdrop for Riya's journey towards work-life balance. Riya was a talented architect who had always been deeply passionate about her craft. She poured her heart and soul into her work, striving for excellence in every project she took on.

As Riya's career soared to new heights, she found herself grappling with the demands of her profession. Long hours at the office and tight project deadlines left little time for self-care and personal pursuits. Riya's family and friends noticed her exhaustion, and they began to worry about her well-being.

One evening, as Riya stood on the rooftop of her apartment, overlooking the breathtaking skyline of Jaipur, she received a call from her childhood friend, Aarav. Aarav was a seasoned traveler who had explored the far corners of the world, seeking wisdom and adventure. He had always been fascinated by the art of finding balance in life, and he could sense the strain in Riya's voice.

"Riya, my dear friend," Aarav said warmly, "I can see that you're struggling to find harmony in your life. Remember, the key to true success lies in balancing your passions and well-being."

Riya sighed, feeling a mix of gratitude and confusion. She knew that Aarav's words held wisdom, but she wasn't sure how to apply them to her life. With Aarav's encouragement, she decided to embark on a transformative journey of self-discovery and resilience.

Riya began by reconnecting with her passions beyond architecture. She had always loved painting, and she found solace in the vibrant art scene of Jaipur. Taking time to paint allowed her to express herself creatively and served as a therapeutic escape from the demands of her career.

One of the most significant challenges for Riya was setting boundaries in her work life. She realized that she needed to communicate her limitations to her clients and colleagues to avoid burnout. As she established clear boundaries, she felt a sense of empowerment and control over her time and energy.

Jaipur's rich cultural heritage offered Riya a unique opportunity for self-care. She immersed herself in the city's traditions, attending colourful festivals, and savouring local delicacies. Embracing the spirit of Jaipur allowed her to find joy in the little moments and appreciate life beyond work.

Riya cherished her family deeply, and she wanted to be present for them despite her demanding career. She learned to prioritize family time and create cherished memories with her loved ones. This brought her a sense of fulfilment and strengthened her emotional resilience.

Riya discovered the power of mindfulness through a chance encounter with a yoga retreat in the outskirts of Jaipur. Practicing yoga and meditation helped her cultivate a sense of calm and presence, which she carried into her daily life. It allowed her to focus on the present moment and approach challenges with clarity.

Riya surrounded herself with supportive friends and mentors who encouraged her on her journey. She sought advice from experienced architects who had achieved a healthy work-life balance. Their guidance and encouragement were invaluable in helping her stay on track.

As Riya encountered obstacles in both her personal and professional life, she relied on grit and a growth mindset to navigate through them. She saw setbacks as opportunities for learning and growth, which allowed her to bounce back with renewed determination.

Riya made her well-being a priority, incorporating daily walks in Jaipur's lush gardens and dedicating time to pursue hobbies. She recognized that taking care of herself was essential to maintaining resilience and sustaining her passion for architecture.

With guidance from a local meditation teacher, Riya deepened her mindfulness practice. She discovered the beauty of meditation in the early morning hours, watching the sun rise over Jaipur's majestic palaces. It brought her a profound sense of inner peace and balance.

As Riya's journey unfolded, she learned to embrace her imperfections and let go of the need for perfection. In architecture and in life, she realized that imperfections were what made things unique and beautiful.

With time, Riya's life transformed. She found harmony in the chaos of Jaipur, proving that resilience and work-life balance were achievable even in the most demanding environments. Her journey was a testament to the power of self-discovery, mindfulness, and supportive relationships in navigating life's turbulence with grace and strength.

The streets of Jaipur witnessed Riya's transformation as she became a beacon of inspiration for others seeking to unleash their resilience and embrace a life of harmony and fulfilment. Her story touched the hearts of many, and her newfound balance enriched not only her life but the lives of those around her.

"
LET THY FOOD BE THY MEDICINE,
AND THY MEDICINE BE THY FOOD."

– HIPPOCRATES

6 Fuelling Resilience - Mindful Nutrition

In the pursuit of resilience, we often overlook the essential role of nutrition in shaping our mental and physical well-being. Food is not merely a source of sustenance; it can be a powerful tool to fuel our resilience and fortify our minds and bodies. The ancient wisdom of "you are what you eat" holds true as our food choices can significantly impact our ability to cope with life's challenges.

Mindful Nutrition is not about restrictive diets or fleeting trends; it is about cultivating a deeper understanding of the profound connection between what we eat and how we feel. Nourishing our bodies with the right nutrients can unlock a new level of resilience, enhancing our capacity to bounce back from setbacks and adapt to the ever-changing circumstances of life.

The journey towards mindful nutrition is not just about what's on our plates but also how we approach and experience food. It involves savoring the flavours, embracing culinary diversity, and acknowledging the sacredness of nourishment. Let us embark on this enlightening voyage to discover the transformative power of mindful nutrition and its role in unlocking the resilience within us.

The Art of Mindful Eating

In the fast-paced world we inhabit, mealtimes are often hurried affairs. We rush through our meals, hardly paying attention to the food we consume. In the process, we lose touch with the innate wisdom of our bodies and fail to listen to its signals of hunger and satiety. The art of mindful eating invites us to slow down and savor every morsel, bringing our full attention to the experience of nourishment.

Mindful eating is not just about chewing slowly or putting down our utensils between bites; it is about engaging all our senses in the act of eating. By immersing ourselves in the colors, textures, aromas, and flavors of our food, we forge a deeper connection with the nourishment that sustains us.

This section explores the transformative practice of mindful eating and its role in building a more resilient relationship with food. From reconnecting with our body's hunger cues to breaking free from emotional eating patterns, we will uncover the secrets of mindful nourishment.

The Healing Power of Nutrient-Dense Foods

Food is more than a sum of calories; it is a source of life-giving nutrients that play a crucial role in our physical and emotional well-being. The foods we choose to consume can either enhance our resilience or hinder it. This section delves into the healing power of nutrient-dense foods and their ability to fortify our bodies against the storms of life.

We will explore a plethora of vibrant, plant-based foods that are rich in antioxidants, vitamins, and minerals. From the vibrant hues of fruits and vegetables to the nourishing goodness of whole grains and legumes, we will unlock the nutritional treasures that nature has bestowed upon us.

Nurturing the Gut-Brain Connection

The gut-brain connection is a profound and intricate relationship that impacts our emotional and mental resilience. Our gut is home to a vast ecosystem of microorganisms that influence not only our digestion but also our mood and mental health. When we nurture our gut with the right foods, we foster a harmonious relationship between our gut and brain, enhancing our resilience in the face of stress and adversity.

In this section, we will delve into the fascinating world of the gut-brain axis and explore the foods that promote gut health and emotional well-being. From fermented foods teeming with probiotics to prebiotic-rich fibres, we will uncover the keys to nurturing this vital connection.

Mindful Nutrition for Stress Management

Stress is an inevitable part of life, but how we nourish ourselves can significantly impact our response to stressors. This section focuses on using mindful nutrition as a tool for stress management. By incorporating stress-busting foods and adopting mindful eating practices, we can build our resilience to cope with life's pressures.

We will delve into the calming properties of certain foods and explore how they influence our stress hormones. Moreover, we will learn to distinguish between emotional hunger and true physical hunger, empowering ourselves to make conscious food choices that soothe our souls and nourish our bodies.

Food Rituals for Resilience

Cultures around the world have long recognized the power of food rituals in fostering resilience and well-being. In this section, we will celebrate the wisdom of traditional food practices and explore how we can incorporate them into our modern lives.

From mindful meal preparation to the mindful consumption of food, we will discover the beauty of food rituals and their potential to elevate our relationship with nutrition. Through time-honored practices, we can infuse our meals with gratitude, intention, and a deeper appreciation for the sustenance they provide.

Nourishing Resilience

As we conclude this journey into mindful nutrition and its role in fuelling resilience, let us pause to reflect on the profound impact our food choices can have on our lives. Mindful nutrition is not a quick fix or a fad diet; it is a way of life that honours the interconnectedness of our bodies, minds, and spirits. It is a journey of self-discovery, where we learn to listen to our bodies' wisdom and make conscious choices that support our well-being.

In the hustle and bustle of our daily lives, it is easy to overlook the significance of what we put on our plates. But by embracing mindful nutrition, we can transform our relationship with food and unlock the resilience that lies within us.

Let us nourish ourselves not just with the physical nutrients but also with the richness of the present moment, the joy of savouring each bite, and the gratitude for the abundance that surrounds us.

As we embrace mindful nutrition in our lives, may we remember that resilience is not just about bouncing back from challenges but also about thriving in the face of adversity. It is about cultivating an unshakable foundation of well-being that allows us to navigate life's turbulence with grace and strength. With every mindful choice we make, we fuel our resilience and create a ripple effect of positive change in our lives and the lives of those around us. Let us embark on this journey of nourishment and self-discovery, for it is through mindful nutrition that we can truly unleash the full potential of our resilience.

let us take a moment to appreciate the wisdom of mindful nutrition and its ability to nourish not only our bodies but also our souls. As we savor the flavours of life, may we remember that resilience is not just a destination but an ever-evolving journey of growth and empowerment.

Let these insights guide us as we continue to unlock the power of resilience within us, step by step, nourishment by nourishment. For in the realm of mindful nutrition, we find not only physical sustenance but also a path to deeper connection, greater awareness, and a more vibrant and resilient way of being.

As we move forward on this journey, let us carry the wisdom of mindful nutrition in our hearts, knowing that with every bite, we nourish not only our bodies but also our capacity to thrive in the dance of life.

In the words of an ancient proverb, "The key to resilience lies in the mindful embrace of nourishment – for within every morsel, we find the sustenance for our souls to soar."

The Gut-Brain Connection

Nurturing Resilience from Within

Deep within the confines of our bodies lies a profound and intricate relationship between our gut and our brain. While we often think of the brain as the centre of intelligence and decision-making, recent scientific discoveries have revealed that the gut plays a pivotal role in shaping not only our physical health but also our emotional well-being and mental resilience.

The gut-brain connection, also known as the gut-brain axis, is a bidirectional communication system that involves a complex network of nerves, hormones, and chemicals. It allows the brain and the gut to constantly exchange information, influencing each other's function and performance.

Understanding the Gut-Brain Connection

The gut, often referred to as the "second brain," is a vast and intricate ecosystem of trillions of microorganisms, including bacteria, viruses, and fungi, collectively known as the gut microbiota. These microorganisms play a crucial role in various bodily functions, such as digestion, nutrient absorption, and immune system regulation.

The gut is also home to the enteric nervous system (ENS), which consists of over 100 million nerve cells lining the gastrointestinal tract. The ENS acts as an independent nervous system, capable of processing information and initiating reflexes without direct input from the brain.

On the other hand, the brain, as the central command centre, governs our thoughts, emotions, and behaviours. It communicates with the gut through the vagus nerve, a long cranial nerve that serves as the main conduit of the gut-brain axis.

The gut and the brain communicate through a complex network of neurotransmitters, hormones, and immune signalling molecules. For instance, the gut produces serotonin, a neurotransmitter commonly associated with mood regulation. In fact, around 90% of the body's serotonin is produced in the gut.

Similarly, the gut microbiota plays a vital role in producing various neurotransmitters and neuroactive compounds, which can influence brain function and mood. The composition of the gut microbiota is influenced by various factors, such as diet, lifestyle, stress, and medication, and in turn, can impact the brain and mental health.

Implications for Resilience

The profound interplay between the gut and the brain has significant implications for our resilience and well-being. Research has shown that a healthy gut-brain axis is crucial for maintaining emotional balance, managing stress, and building mental resilience.

1. Emotional Regulation: The gut-brain connection influences how we process emotions and respond to stress. A well-balanced gut microbiota can enhance emotional regulation and reduce the risk of mood disorders such as anxiety and depression.

2. Stress Response: Chronic stress can disrupt the gut-brain axis, leading to digestive issues and imbalances in the gut microbiota. On the other hand, a healthy gut can enhance the body's stress response and help buffer against the negative effects of stress.

3. Cognitive Function: The gut-brain axis also impacts cognitive function, including memory, learning, and decision-making. A healthy gut can support optimal brain function and cognitive performance.

4. Inflammation and Immunity: The gut microbiota plays a crucial role in regulating the immune system and controlling inflammation. Chronic inflammation can negatively affect both gut and brain health, while a balanced gut microbiota can support a healthy immune system and reduce inflammation.

5. Resilience to Mental Health Disorders: Emerging evidence suggests that the gut-brain axis may play a role in the development and resilience to mental health disorders. A healthy gut environment can enhance resilience and reduce the risk of mental health challenges.

Nurturing the Gut-Brain Connection

Given the vital role of the gut-brain axis in fostering resilience and well-being, it becomes essential to prioritize the health of our gut. Here are some strategies to nurture the gut-brain connection and support mental resilience:

1. A Balanced Diet: Consuming a diverse and nutrient-rich diet supports a healthy gut microbiota. Include a variety of fruits, vegetables, whole grains, and probiotic-rich foods such as yogurt and fermented vegetables.

2. Mindful Eating: Practice mindful eating by savoring each bite, chewing slowly, and paying attention to the sensory experience of eating. Mindful eating can enhance digestion and promote a sense of well-being.

3. Regular Exercise: Physical activity has been shown to positively impact the gut microbiota and support brain health. Engage in regular exercise to nurture both your gut and your brain.

4. Stress Management: Chronic stress can disrupt the gut-brain axis, so it's essential to manage stress through techniques such as meditation, deep breathing, yoga, and spending time in nature.

5. Adequate Sleep: Prioritize quality sleep, as it plays a crucial role in supporting gut health and brain function.

6. Limiting Antibiotics: While antibiotics can be life-saving, overuse can disrupt the gut microbiota. Use antibiotics judiciously and consider probiotics to support gut health during and after antibiotic treatment.

7. Probiotic Supplements: Probiotics are live beneficial bacteria that can help maintain a healthy gut microbiota. Consult with a qualified healthcare professional before starting any probiotic supplement to ensure it aligns with your specific health needs.

8. Avoiding Toxins: Minimize exposure to toxins and pollutants that can negatively impact the gut microbiota. Choose organic foods whenever possible and use natural cleaning and personal care products.

9. Cultivating Mindfulness: Mindfulness practices, such as meditation and deep breathing exercises, can reduce stress and promote a harmonious gut-brain connection.

10. Social Connections: Strong social connections and positive relationships have been linked to a healthier gut microbiota and better mental health. Nurture your social connections and surround yourself with supportive individuals.

The gut-brain connection is a fascinating and complex phenomenon that underscores the importance of a holistic approach to resilience and well-being. By nourishing our bodies and minds through mindful nutrition, stress management, and positive lifestyle choices, we can strengthen the gut-brain axis and cultivate a deeper sense of resilience in the face of life's challenges. Embracing the profound connection between our gut and our brain allows us to unlock the potential for a healthier, happier, and more resilient life.

In the journey of unleashing resilience, Chapter 6 serves as a crucial stepping stone, urging us to embrace the power of mindful nutrition to fuel our minds and bodies. As we continue on this transformative path, let us remember that every bite we take and every moment of mindful presence can contribute to the intricate symphony of our gut-brain connection, shaping our resilience, and empowering us to navigate life's turbulence with grace and strength.

With each chapter we delve into, we peel back the layers of what it means to be truly resilient. As we embrace self-discovery, harness the power of positivity, and cultivate inner strength, we find ourselves standing firm amidst life's storms.

let us embark on this extraordinary odyssey of resilience—a journey that will lead us to the depths of our own souls, where strength, courage, and resilience intertwine. As we weave our way through life's kaleidoscope of experiences, may we emerge brighter, bolder, and more resilient than ever before. For it is in the tapestry of our struggles and triumphs that the true beauty of resilience is revealed.

As we take these words to heart and embrace the wisdom they hold, let us step boldly into the uncharted territory of resilience. Let us face life's challenges with unwavering determination and unyielding courage, knowing that within us lies the power to rise, to heal, and to thrive.

For when we unleash resilience, we not only transform ourselves, but we also touch the lives of others, igniting a ripple effect of strength and hope that transcends time and space.

So, dear reader, I invite you to embark on this transformative journey—a journey of self-discovery, growth, and resilience. As we turn the pages of this book, may we find inspiration, guidance, and solace in the power of resilience—the extraordinary force that resides within us all.

In the words of an ancient proverb: "The bamboo that bends is stronger than the oak that resists." Let us be like the bamboo, bending and swaying with life's winds, yet standing tall and resolute in our inner strength.

Let this be the beginning of a remarkable expedition—a journey of resilience, growth, and transformation. And as we navigate the intricacies of life's kaleidoscope, may we remember that within us lies the power to unleash our resilience and create an extraordinary life—one that dances with destiny, embraces synchronicities, and resounds with the symphony of resilience.

Nutritional Strategies for Resilience

In the pursuit of unleashing resilience, one of the most crucial and often overlooked aspects is the role of nutrition. What we put into our bodies has a profound impact on our physical health, mental well-being, and overall resilience. In this section, we will explore the power of nutritional strategies in fortifying our bodies and minds to navigate life's challenges with greater strength and grace.

1. Nourishing the Body: The Foundation of Resilience

At the heart of resilience lies a well-nourished body. Just as a strong foundation supports a sturdy building, proper nutrition provides the groundwork for a resilient mind and body. A balanced diet rich in essential nutrients, vitamins, and minerals is essential to support our immune system, regulate our hormones, and maintain optimal brain function. Whole foods, such as fruits, vegetables, whole grains, lean proteins, and healthy fats, form the cornerstone of a resilient diet.

2. Mindful Eating: Cultivating Awareness and Connection

In a fast-paced world, the act of eating has become more of a rushed necessity than a mindful practice. However, approaching meals with mindfulness can profoundly impact our relationship with food and, subsequently, our resilience. Mindful eating involves savoring each bite, paying attention to hunger and fullness cues, and fostering a deeper connection with the food we consume. By slowing down and savoring our meals, we can better nourish our bodies and cultivate a sense of gratitude for the sustenance we receive.

3. Gut Health: The Second Brain

Emerging research has unveiled the intricate connection between our gut and our brain—the so-called "second brain." The gut-brain axis plays a significant role in regulating mood, emotions, and stress response. A healthy gut microbiome, fostered through a diet rich in probiotics and prebiotics, can promote emotional resilience and mental well-being. Fermented foods, such as yogurt, kefir, sauerkraut, and kimchi, are excellent sources of probiotics, while prebiotic foods like garlic, onions, and bananas support the growth of beneficial gut bacteria.

4. The Power of Antioxidants: Fighting Oxidative Stress

Oxidative stress, caused by an imbalance of free radicals and antioxidants in the body, can lead to cellular damage and contribute to various health issues. Antioxidants, found abundantly in fruits and vegetables, play a crucial role in neutralizing free radicals and reducing oxidative stress. By incorporating a rainbow of colourful fruits and vegetables into our diet, we can bolster our antioxidant defences and protect our cells from damage, thus promoting resilience at the cellular level.

5. Omega-3 Fatty Acids: Nourishing the Brain

Omega-3 fatty acids are essential fats that play a vital role in brain health and cognitive function. They are found in fatty fish, flaxseeds, chia seeds, and walnuts, among other sources. These healthy fats support the structure of brain cells, enhance neurotransmitter function, and may even help reduce inflammation in the brain. Including omega-3-rich foods in our diet can enhance our cognitive resilience and mental clarity.

6. Hydration: The Elixir of Life

Often underestimated, hydration is a fundamental aspect of resilience. Dehydration can lead to fatigue, impaired cognitive function, and decreased physical performance. Staying adequately hydrated supports our body's natural detoxification processes, helps regulate body temperature, and ensures that our cells function optimally. Drinking water throughout the day is a simple yet powerful way to fuel our bodies and minds.

7. Mind-Gut Connection: Eating for Emotional Well-being

The foods we eat not only impact our physical health but also influence our emotional well-being. Certain foods, such as sugary and processed treats, may provide temporary pleasure but can lead to energy crashes and mood swings. On the other hand, nutrient-dense foods rich in vitamins, minerals, and amino acids can promote stable moods and emotional resilience. By nurturing our bodies with wholesome foods, we foster a positive mind-gut connection, promoting emotional balance and overall resilience.

8. Caffeine and Alcohol: Striking a Balance

and alcohol are common elements in many people's lives, but their consumption can impact our resilience. While moderate amounts of caffeine can provide a temporary boost in energy and alertness, excessive intake can lead to jitteriness and disrupt sleep. Similarly, while occasional alcohol consumption may be enjoyable for some, excessive drinking can negatively affect sleep quality, mood, and overall health. Striking a balance and being mindful of our intake can help us maintain resilience and well-being.

9. The Role of Supplements: Bridging Nutritional Gaps

In an ideal world, all our nutritional needs would be met through a balanced diet. However, various factors, such as dietary preferences, lifestyle constraints, and health conditions, may lead to nutritional gaps. In such cases, supplements can play a role in supporting our resilience. However, it is crucial to consult with a qualified healthcare professional before starting any supplement regimen to ensure that it aligns with our individual health needs.

10. Sustainable Nutrition: Caring for Ourselves and the Planet

Resilience is not only about caring for ourselves but also extends to caring for the world around us. Embracing sustainable nutrition practices, such as choosing locally sourced and seasonal foods, reducing food waste, and opting for eco-friendly packaging, can contribute to our resilience and the resilience of the planet. By nourishing ourselves in harmony with nature, we create a symbiotic relationship that benefits both our well-being and the health of the Earth.

In this chapter, we have explored the profound impact of nutrition on our resilience—how nourishing our bodies with wholesome foods can strengthen our physical health, support our mental well-being, and empower us to navigate life's turbulence with greater ease. As we continue on this journey of unleashing resilience, let us remember that the power to fuel our resilience lies within our own hands, with each choice we make at the dining table.

As we nourish ourselves with intention and mindfulness, we nourish the very essence of resilience—the extraordinary force that resides within us all. In the words of an ancient proverb: "A well-nourished body, a well-nourished mind; resilience thrives, and life's storms unwind."

Eating for Energy and Mental Clarity

In the fast-paced world we inhabit, it is common to experience fatigue, mental fog, and a lack of focus. In this section, we will delve into the vital connection between what we eat and our energy levels and mental clarity. By understanding the role of nutrition in enhancing vitality and cognitive function, we can harness the power of food to fuel our resilience and thrive in every aspect of life.

1. The Energy Equation: Understanding the Source

Energy is the life force that propels us forward, allowing us to accomplish tasks, engage with others, and pursue our passions. However, the source of our energy goes beyond mere calories—it lies in the nutrients we consume. High-energy foods, such as complex carbohydrates, proteins, and healthy fats, provide a sustained and steady source of vitality. In contrast, sugary and processed foods may offer a quick surge of energy but lead to subsequent crashes, leaving us drained and fatigued.

2. Fueling with Complex Carbohydrates

Complex carbohydrates are a cornerstone of sustained energy and mental clarity. These carbohydrates break down slowly, releasing glucose into our bloodstream at a steady pace. Foods such as whole grains, sweet potatoes, and legumes provide a stable source of energy, ensuring that we remain alert and focused throughout the day. Incorporating complex carbs into our meals and snacks can enhance our resilience, keeping us energized and clear-headed.

3. Protein-Power: Building Blocks for Vitality

Proteins are the building blocks of life, and they play a crucial role in replenishing and repairing our bodies. In the context of energy and mental clarity, proteins support the steady release of energy from carbohydrates and help maintain stable blood sugar levels. Moreover, certain amino acids found in protein-rich foods are essential for neurotransmitter production, enhancing our cognitive function. Lean meats, fish, dairy, tofu, and plant-based protein sources offer an array of options to power our resilience.

4. The Role of Healthy Fats

The idea of fats promoting energy might seem counterintuitive, but healthy fats are an essential part of a resilient diet. Omega-3 fatty acids, found in fatty fish, flaxseeds, and walnuts, are particularly beneficial for brain health and cognitive function. These fats help reduce inflammation in the brain and support the transmission of nerve signals, enhancing mental clarity and focus. Including sources of healthy fats in our meals can provide a stable and sustained source of energy for both the body and mind.

5. Mindful Eating for Energy

In a world filled with distractions, it is easy to fall into mindless eating patterns. Mindful eating, on the other hand, encourages us to savor each bite, pay attention to hunger and satiety cues, and cultivate a deeper appreciation for the nourishment we receive. By practicing mindful eating, we can better tune into our body's energy needs and make conscious choices that support our resilience.

6. Hydration: The Fountain of Energy

Amidst busy schedules, hydration often takes a backseat. However, staying well-hydrated is vital for maintaining energy levels and mental clarity. Dehydration can lead to fatigue, reduced cognitive function, and impaired physical performance. Drinking water throughout the day not only keeps us energized but also aids in detoxification and supports the body's natural processes.

7. Nourishing Snack Ideas for Sustained Energy

Snacking can be an opportunity to refuel and recharge. Instead of reaching for sugary and processed snacks, we can opt for nutrient-dense alternatives that provide sustained energy. A handful of mixed nuts, a piece of whole fruit, yogurt with berries, or carrot sticks with hummus are examples of nourishing snacks that can help us stay energized and mentally alert.

8. The Role of Caffeine and Herbal Teas

Caffeine is a widely consumed stimulant that can provide a temporary boost in energy and focus. While moderate amounts of caffeine can be beneficial for some individuals, excessive intake may lead to jitteriness, anxiety, and disrupted sleep patterns. Herbal teas, such as green tea and chamomile tea, offer a gentler alternative to support relaxation and mental clarity.

9. Understanding Energy Balance

Beyond the foods we eat, energy balance is crucial for resilience. Balancing energy expenditure with energy intake ensures that we have enough fuel to meet the demands of our daily lives. Regular physical activity, sufficient sleep, and stress management all play essential roles in maintaining energy balance and supporting our overall well-being.

10. Cultivating Long-Term Resilience

Sustainable energy and mental clarity are not only about quick fixes but rather the cumulative impact of our lifestyle choices. By adopting nourishing eating habits, staying hydrated, and engaging in regular physical activity, we can cultivate long-term resilience and vitality. Embracing a holistic approach to nourishing our bodies and minds empowers us to navigate life's challenges with vigor and clarity.

Wise words of an ancient proverb: "Nourish your body, ignite your soul; with energy and clarity, resilience takes control."

"
IN THE DARKEST OF STORMS,
RESILIENCE BECOMES OUR ANCHOR,
GUIDING US THROUGH THE CHAOS TO CALMER SHORES. "

7 Resilience in Crisis

Rising Above the Storm

Amidst the darkest of days and the fiercest of storms, the human spirit finds its truest expression – resilience. It is in these crucibles of crisis that we are tested, pushed to the brink of our limits, and yet, somehow, we find the strength to rise above the tempests that threaten to engulf us. The journey to resilience in crisis is not one of smooth seas and clear skies; rather, it is a tumultuous voyage of self-discovery, where we are forced to confront our deepest fears and vulnerabilities.

In the heart of chaos, emotions swirl like the raging winds, tossing us about with uncertainty and doubt. Fear grips our hearts, threatening to paralyze us, and the weight of the unknown bears down upon us. It is in these moments of vulnerability that we must find the courage to face our fears head-on. Resilience does not mean an absence of fear; it is the ability to acknowledge our fears and move forward despite them.

When faced with crisis, we are often compelled to retreat into the safety of what is familiar, clinging desperately to the fragments of normalcy that remain. Yet, it is in surrendering to the uncertainty of the unknown that we find the power to transcend the storm. Like a phoenix rising from the ashes, we emerge from the depths of crisis transformed, reborn into a new version of ourselves.

The journey to resilience Is not a solitary one; It Is one that we must undertake together. In times of crisis, we draw strength from the support and love of our community. Like a tightly knit net, they catch us when we fall, offering a glimmer of hope in the darkest of hours. The bonds of solidarity remind us that we are not alone, that we are interconnected, and that our collective resilience is greater than the sum of its parts.

Amidst the chaos, we seek solace in the quiet corners of our minds. Mindfulness becomes our refuge, a sanctuary of stillness amidst the chaos. In the depths of crisis, it is easy to become overwhelmed by the noise and distractions, but mindfulness offers us a lifeline back to the present moment. It is in this present awareness that we find clarity, the ability to discern what is within our control and what is not.

Resilience in crisis is not about finding quick fixes or easy solutions; it is a journey of introspection and self-compassion. We must learn to be gentle with ourselves, to forgive ourselves for our perceived shortcomings and mistakes. The path to resilience is paved with self-acceptance, a deep-rooted belief that we are worthy of love and care, even in the midst of chaos.

In times of crisis, we are often forced to confront the impermanence of life, the fragility of our existence. This confrontation can be unnerving, but it is also a catalyst for growth and transformation. When we embrace the impermanence of life, we open ourselves up to the possibility of change and renewal. We learn to let go of what no longer serves us, and in doing so, we create space for new beginnings.

The journey to resilience Is not linear; It Is a dance of progress and setbacks, of triumphs and failures. It is in the moments of adversity that our resilience is truly tested, and it is through these challenges that we learn the most profound lessons. Resilience is not about being invincible; it is about finding the strength to rise each time we fall.

In the chapters that follow, we will explore the multifaceted nature of resilience in crisis. We will dive deep into the wellsprings of human strength and uncover the tools and strategies that enable us to rise above the storms. Each section will be a testament to the indomitable spirit that resides within us, a reminder that even amidst the darkest of days, we have the power to find our way back to the light.

Resilience is not a destination; it is a way of life. It is the unwavering commitment to self-growth, the relentless pursuit of inner strength, and the unyielding belief in our capacity to weather life's storms. As we embark on this journey together, let us remember that within each of us lies the power to rise above the storm, to unleash the extraordinary resilience that resides within. For it is in the crucible of crisis that we discover the true essence of our being – the boundless courage, the unshakeable hope, and the enduring spirit that enables us to rise, again and again, above life's tumultuous seas.

Coping with Trauma

In the bustling city of Mumbai, where life moves at a frenetic pace, lived Aryan Sharma, a gifted musician whose soulful tunes connected with the hearts of many. He had just finished a spectacular concert with his bandmates and friends when the unthinkable happened - a deafening explosion ripped through the crowd, shattering Aryan's world.

The Night That Changed Everything

The night was etched in Aryan's memory like a never-ending nightmare. Amidst the chaos and panic, he struggled to comprehend what had happened. The once joyous celebration turned into a scene of unimaginable horror. The blast had taken away his friends, bandmates, and any sense of security he had known.

A Ray of Light in Darkness

As Aryan lay in the hospital bed, physical pain merging with emotional turmoil, he felt a gentle presence beside him. Dr. Raj Singh, a seasoned psychologist with eyes that held both empathy and strength, stood by his side. Dr. Raj became a lifeline for Aryan, helping him navigate the storm of emotions that threatened to drown him.

Unravelling the Layers

In the safety of Dr. Raj's office, Aryan found solace in opening up about the trauma he had endured. He delved into the depths of his emotions, unpacking the guilt, fear, and anger that engulfed him. Dr. Raj listened without judgment, guiding him through the intricate web of his thoughts and feelings.

Weaving New Threads of Trust

Aryan's journey of healing was not a solitary one. His elder sister, Priya, a beacon of unwavering support, encouraged him to lean on her during his darkest moments. Priya reminded him that it was okay to ask for help and that true strength lay in vulnerability. Slowly, Aryan began to rebuild his trust in the world around him.

Embracing the Fragility

In therapy, Aryan learned that resilience was not about denying vulnerability but rather embracing it. Dr. Raj introduced him to mindfulness practices that anchored him to the present, guiding him away from the trauma's haunting memories. Through meditation, Aryan discovered moments of clarity amidst the emotional turbulence.

The Power of Shared Healing

Through group therapy, Aryan met others who had experienced their own versions of trauma. As they shared their stories, a profound sense of connection emerged. Each person's journey of resilience intertwined, forming a tapestry of support and understanding. Together, they found strength in their shared vulnerability.

Melodies of Resilience

Aryan's music, once a means of escape, now became an instrument of healing. The melodies he composed were woven from the threads of his pain, love, and hope. As he poured his heart into each note, he discovered the therapeutic power of his art.

Epilogue: Echoes of Resilience

Aryan's path to healing was marked by ups and downs, but he refused to let his trauma define him. Instead, he used his music to create a resonating echo of resilience. Through performances and workshops, he reached out to communities affected by trauma, offering them a message of hope and healing.

In the heart of Mumbai, amidst the bustling chaos, Aryan's music became a symbol of resilience and unity. His story, a testament to the human spirit's capacity to endure and transform, touched the lives of many. Aryan's journey taught us that even in the face of unimaginable darkness, there is always a glimmer of light within, waiting to guide us towards healing and resilience.

Coping with Trauma: Embracing Healing and Resilience

Trauma is an uninvited guest that can shatter our lives, leaving behind emotional wounds that seem impossible to heal. Whether it stems from a devastating event, a loss, or prolonged exposure to distressing experiences, trauma has the power to overwhelm and reshape our sense of self. Coping with trauma requires navigating through the labyrinth of emotions, memories, and physical sensations that can linger long after the actual event has passed.

Understanding Trauma

Trauma is not a singular experience; it is a deeply personal response to distressing events. Its impact can be immediate or delayed, manifesting as a flood of emotions or a numb detachment. Understanding trauma is the first step towards healing. It is essential to recognize that there is no right or wrong way to respond to trauma - everyone copes differently.

The Rollercoaster of Emotions

One of the most overwhelming aspects of coping with trauma is the rollercoaster of emotions it brings. Fear, anger, guilt, and sadness may coexist within, leaving individuals feeling like they are on an emotional tightrope. Acknowledging these emotions and giving ourselves permission to feel them without judgment is a vital part of the healing process.

Navigating the Aftermath

In the aftermath of trauma, life can feel chaotic and disorienting. Flashbacks, nightmares, and intrusive thoughts may plague survivors, making it challenging to engage in daily activities. It is crucial to create a safe and supportive environment, seeking professional help if needed. Therapy and counselling provide a safe space to explore emotions and gain tools to cope with trauma's impact.

Embracing Resilience

Resilience is the inner strength that enables us to weather life's storms. While trauma can leave scars, it does not define our future. Embracing resilience means acknowledging the trauma's impact while recognizing the potential for growth and healing. Building resilience involves fostering positive coping strategies and seeking support from loved ones and professionals.

Mindfulness as an Anchor

Practicing mindfulness can provide an anchor amidst the turbulent waters of trauma. Mindfulness helps individuals stay grounded in the present moment, preventing them from being overwhelmed by past memories or future anxieties. Techniques like deep breathing, body scans, and meditation can be powerful tools in restoring a sense of balance and control.

Reconnecting with Others

Trauma can lead individuals to withdraw from others, believing that they are a burden or that no one can understand their pain. Reconnecting with loved ones and supportive friends is an essential step in the healing process. Genuine connections and empathy help survivors feel less isolated and reinforce the belief that they are not alone in their journey.

The Journey of Self-Compassion

Practicing self-compassion is a transformative journey towards healing. It involves treating ourselves with the same kindness and understanding we would offer a friend in pain. Self-compassion acknowledges that we are human and allows us to embrace our vulnerabilities without self-judgment.

Seeking Professional Help

Coping with trauma can be a challenging and complex process. Seeking professional help from therapists, counselors, or support groups can be a vital step in the healing journey. Professionals offer a safe space to explore emotions, process trauma, and gain tools to cope with its effects.

Finding Meaning and Purpose

As survivors progress on their healing journey, they may find meaning and purpose in their experiences. Some individuals may choose to use their trauma as a catalyst for change, advocating for others or using their experiences to inspire art, writing, or other forms of creative expression.

Rediscovering Joy and Hope

While coping with trauma is a profound and transformative process, it is also about rediscovering joy and hope. Despite the darkness that trauma may bring, there is light on the other side. Finding joy in simple pleasures, embracing hope for the future, and celebrating even the smallest victories are essential in this journey.

The Path of Resilience

Coping with trauma is a courageous journey of healing and resilience. It is a testament to the human spirit's capacity to endure, grow, and transform. By acknowledging the pain, seeking support, and nurturing resilience, survivors can find strength in their vulnerability and rebuild their lives with newfound purpose and meaning.

Adapting to Sudden Changes

Embracing Flexibility and Resilience

Life is an unpredictable journey, and at times, it throws unexpected challenges our way. Sudden changes can be daunting, leaving us feeling unprepared and anxious. However, our ability to adapt and remain resilient in the face of these changes can make all the difference. Adapting to sudden changes requires a mindset of flexibility and a willingness to embrace the unknown. In this section, we will explore the art of adapting to sudden changes and how it can lead to personal growth and a deeper sense of resilience.

1. Embracing the Unpredictability of Life

Life's journey is filled with twists and turns, and sudden changes are an inherent part of it. Embracing the unpredictability of life allows us to let go of the illusion of control and be open to new possibilities. Instead of resisting change, we can choose to flow with it, understanding that even in uncertainty lies the potential for growth.

2. Letting Go of Resistance

When faced with sudden changes, it is natural to resist and cling to the familiar. However, resistance only prolongs our suffering and prevents us from moving forward. Letting go of resistance involves acknowledging our emotions and fears while gently releasing our grip on what was. By doing so, we create space for new experiences and opportunities to unfold.

3. Cultivating Resilience in the Face of Adversity

Resilience is the backbone of our ability to adapt. It is the inner strength that enables us to bounce back from challenges and find new paths forward. Cultivating resilience involves developing coping strategies, seeking support from others, and finding meaning and purpose in difficult circumstances.

4. Staying Grounded in the Present

In times of sudden change, our minds can often race with worries about the future or regrets about the past. Staying grounded in the present moment can help us find stability amidst the turbulence. Mindfulness practices, such as meditation and deep breathing, can anchor us to the here and now, allowing us to respond to changes with clarity and composure.

5. Finding Opportunity in Change

While sudden changes can be disorienting, they also present opportunities for growth and transformation. By reframing our perspective, we can view change as a chance to learn, evolve, and expand our horizons. Embracing change as an opportunity can ignite creativity and pave the way for new beginnings.

6. Building Flexibility and Adaptability

Flexibility and adaptability are crucial skills in navigating sudden changes. Just as a tree bends with the wind, being flexible allows us to bend without breaking. We can cultivate flexibility by embracing change as an essential part of life and reframing challenges as opportunities to stretch and grow.

7. Seeking Support and Connection

During times of sudden change, reaching out for support can provide a lifeline. Connecting with friends, family, or support groups can help us process our emotions, gain perspective, and find comfort in knowing we are not alone. The power of human connection can be a tremendous source of strength during turbulent times.

8. Accepting Impermanence

Change is an inevitable part of life, and accepting the impermanence of all things can bring a sense of peace and serenity. When we let go of the need to hold onto the past or control the future, we can fully embrace the present moment and find joy in the ever-changing dance of life.

9. Resilience as a Process, Not an Endpoint

Building resilience and adapting to sudden changes is an ongoing process, not a destination. It requires patience, self-compassion, and a willingness to learn from every experience. Each challenge we face becomes an opportunity to strengthen our resilience and deepen our capacity to embrace life's uncertainties.

10. Celebrating Our Strength

As we navigate sudden changes and adapt with resilience, it is essential to acknowledge and celebrate our strength and growth. Celebrating our ability to overcome challenges and embrace change empowers us to face future uncertainties with confidence and grace.

Embracing the Journey

Adapting to sudden changes is a transformative journey of self-discovery and growth. By cultivating flexibility, resilience, and an open heart, we can navigate life's unpredictable terrain with courage and grace. Embracing the journey of adapting to sudden changes allows us to flow with the currents of life, discovering newfound strength and resilience along the way.

Embracing the Storm: A Tale of Adapting to Sudden Changes

In the serene and picturesque village of Uttarakhand, there once lived a man named Keshav, who was known for his deep love and profound connection with nature. He lived a simple life, surrounded by the majestic mountains and lush greenery, finding solace in the tranquillity of the land.

Keshav's life took a heart-wrenching turn when a devastating landslide struck the village, leaving a trail of destruction in its wake. Among the casualties was Keshav's beloved wife, Meera, who was swept away by the force of nature. The loss shattered Keshav's world, leaving him adrift in a sea of grief and sorrow.

The village, too, mourned the loss of Meera, a woman who had brought light and joy to the lives of those around her. In their collective grief, the villagers struggled to find a way forward amidst the debris of their shattered homes and broken spirits.

In the aftermath of the tragedy, Keshav found himself grappling with emotions he had never experienced before. The pain of loss weighed heavily on his heart, and he questioned the very purpose of life. Yet, amid the darkness, a glimmer of hope emerged when he stumbled upon a young sapling that had miraculously survived the landslide.

The sight of the resilient sapling struck a chord in Keshav's heart. It stood as a symbol of hope amidst devastation, a reminder that life could emerge even from the most barren and broken of grounds. In that moment, Keshav realized that his grief could be transformed into something beautiful and meaningful, just like the young sapling before him.

With newfound determination, Keshav embarked on a journey of healing and self-discovery. He immersed himself in nature, finding solace in the mountains and streams that had witnessed his love story with Meera. He started tending to the resilient sapling, nurturing it with care and love, just as he had cared for Meera.

As the sapling grew, so did Keshav's strength and resilience. He found comfort in the beauty of nature, witnessing the cycle of life and death, and realizing that loss was an inevitable part of the grand tapestry of existence. He understood that even in the face of loss, life continued to flourish, and he was determined to do the same.

In the village, Keshav's transformation did not go unnoticed. His resilience and ability to find hope in the darkest of times inspired others to find their own strength. Together, they began rebuilding their homes and their lives, each person drawing strength from the resilient sapling that had become a symbol of hope and renewal.

As time passed, the sapling blossomed into a magnificent tree, providing shade and shelter to the village that had embraced it as a beacon of hope. Keshav, too, found his purpose in nurturing not just the tree but also the spirits of those around him.

The tree, which came to be known as the "Tree of Resilience," became a gathering place for the villagers, where they shared stories of loss, love, and life. It became a symbol of their collective strength and an enduring reminder that even in the face of adversity, life could bloom anew.

Keshav's journey of resilience taught the village an invaluable lesson—that in the midst of loss and grief, there was an opportunity for growth and transformation. The Tree of Resilience became a living testament to the power of the human spirit to rise above the storms of life and find meaning, hope, and love in the face of tragedy.

And so, the village of Uttarakhand carried on, forever changed by the wisdom and resilience of one man and the enduring legacy of a tree that stood tall, not only as a memorial to lost lives but as a symbol of life's resilience in the face of its most challenging moments.

Post-Traumatic Growth

Flourishing Amidst Adversity

Life's journey is filled with unpredictable twists and turns, and sometimes, it leads us down paths we never anticipated. At times, we encounter traumatic events that shake the very foundation of our being. While trauma can be immensely challenging, it can also serve as a catalyst for profound personal growth and transformation. This phenomenon is known as post-traumatic growth—a concept that has garnered increasing attention from psychologists and researchers over the years.

Defining Post-Traumatic Growth

Post-traumatic growth is the positive psychological change that individuals experience in the aftermath of adversity or trauma. It is not simply a return to baseline functioning but an opportunity to transcend one's previous state and cultivate newfound strengths and perspectives. Unlike resilience, which focuses on bouncing back to pre-trauma levels, post-traumatic growth emphasizes moving forward with a deeper sense of purpose and resilience.

The Five Domains of Post-Traumatic Growth

Researchers have identified five key domains in which individuals commonly experience post-traumatic growth:

1. Personal Strength: Trauma can challenge individuals to discover untapped reservoirs of inner strength. As they navigate through the storm, they often develop a heightened sense of self-reliance, determination, and courage.

2. Enhanced Relationships: Adversity can bring people closer together. Post-traumatic growth often involves a deepening of existing relationships and the formation of new, meaningful connections with others who have endured similar experiences.

3. Appreciation of Life: Confronting mortality and fragility can lead to a profound appreciation for the beauty and preciousness of life. Individuals may find themselves savoring simple moments and cultivating gratitude for the present.

4. New Possibilities: Trauma can shatter the perception of what is possible. Post-traumatic growth opens individuals to embrace new possibilities, reassess their priorities, and pursue paths they might have once considered unattainable.

5. Spiritual Growth: Navigating adversity often leads individuals to explore questions of meaning, purpose, and spirituality. Post-traumatic growth may involve a deepening of one's spiritual or philosophical beliefs, providing a framework for understanding and finding meaning in the face of suffering.

The Process of Post-Traumatic Growth

Post-traumatic growth is not an instantaneous process but a gradual and complex journey. It often unfolds in stages, with individuals moving through different phases of adaptation and growth.

1. Confronting the Crisis: The first step towards post-traumatic growth is acknowledging and confronting the impact of the trauma. This involves accepting the emotional upheaval and distress it brings.

2. Finding Meaning: As individuals grapple with the aftermath of trauma, they may seek to find meaning in their experiences. This search for meaning can be transformative, providing a sense of purpose and direction.

3. Redefining Identity: Trauma can shake the foundations of one's identity. Post-traumatic growth involves reconstructing a new sense of self that incorporates the experience of trauma as a part of the broader narrative.

4. Cultivating Coping Strategies: To facilitate growth, individuals develop coping strategies to manage the emotional and psychological challenges that arise from trauma. This might involve seeking professional support, engaging in mindfulness practices, or leaning on social support networks.

5. Embracing Growth: As individuals gradually navigate the path of healing, they begin to embrace the growth that emerges from their resilience. This is a transformative process, allowing them to discover newfound strengths and capabilities.

The Role of Resilience

Resilience is a key factor in post-traumatic growth. While trauma can be deeply distressing, resilience equips individuals with the capacity to navigate adversity and find strength in the face of adversity. Resilience involves bouncing back from setbacks, maintaining a positive outlook, and adapting to changing circumstances.

Cultivating Resilience and Post-Traumatic Growth

While post-traumatic growth is a natural process, there are ways to cultivate and foster it intentionally:

1. Embrace Vulnerability: Acknowledging vulnerability is a powerful step towards growth. Opening oneself to the process of healing and growth requires courage and self-compassion.

2. Seek Support: Building a strong support network of family, friends, and mental health professionals can facilitate the journey of post-traumatic growth. Connection and empathy provide a safe space for healing.

3. Practice Self-Reflection: Engaging in self-reflection and journaling can help individuals process their experiences, emotions, and thoughts, leading to greater self-awareness and personal growth.

4. Engage in Mindfulness: Mindfulness practices, such as meditation and deep breathing, can help individuals stay grounded and present in the face of trauma, fostering emotional regulation and resilience.

5. Engage in Meaningful Activities: Pursuing activities that align with personal values and bring joy can facilitate the process of post-traumatic growth, helping individuals reconnect with their sense of purpose.

Post-traumatic growth is a testament to the indomitable human spirit the ability to rise above adversity and transform pain into purpose. While trauma can leave deep scars, it can also sow the seeds of resilience and growth. The journey of post-traumatic growth is a profound and humbling one, illuminating the resilience that resides within each of us and reminding us of the human capacity to thrive amidst life's storms.

A Phoenix's Rise

Overcoming Tragedy with Post-Traumatic Growth

In the serene village of Shantipur, nestled amid the verdant landscapes of southern India, lived a young man named Ravi. His life was one of simplicity and contentment, revolving around his family's small farm and the close-knit community that surrounded him. But, on one fateful day, the tranquillity of Shantipur was shattered by a devastating natural disaster—a powerful cyclone that unleashed its fury upon the village, leaving behind a trail of destruction and heartache.

The Tragedy

The cyclone's wrath spared nothing in its path. Ravi's family home was reduced to rubble, and his parents and younger sister lost their lives in the calamity. The storm tore apart the village, leaving the survivors grappling with grief, trauma, and uncertainty about the future.

In the aftermath of the tragedy, Ravi found himself grappling with overwhelming emotions of loss, guilt, and despair. He felt as if life's entire burden had come crashing down upon his shoulders. He withdrew from the community, seeking solace in isolation, struggling to find meaning amid the chaos.

The Journey of Healing

As the days turned into weeks, the villagers rallied together to rebuild their homes and lives. In the midst of this collective effort, Ravi's neighbors reached out to him, offering their support and compassion. Initially hesitant, he eventually accepted their gestures of kindness, finding comfort in shared sorrow.

One evening, during a community gathering, an elderly man named Guruji shared his own story of loss and resilience. He spoke of his experiences in navigating the aftermath of a devastating earthquake that had struck his hometown decades ago. Guruji's tale of hope amidst adversity resonated deeply with Ravi.

Finding Purpose in the Darkness

Inspired by Guruji's story, Ravi embarked on a journey of self-discovery. He sought guidance from elders, participated in healing circles, and engaged in therapeutic practices. The pain of his loss remained, but Ravi started recognizing the strength that lay dormant within him. He began attending workshops on mindfulness and meditation, embracing these practices as pillars of support in his healing process.

Ravi's connection to nature, instilled in him from his childhood on the family farm, took on a deeper significance. He found solace in tending to the land, nurturing it with care and dedication, mirroring his own journey of growth and renewal. Amidst the fertile fields, he learned that life, even in its darkest moments, had the potential for regeneration and transformation.

The Birth of a New Purpose

As months passed, Ravi's perspective began to shift. He started volunteering at a local support centre for trauma survivors, where he met others who had endured their own tragedies. Ravi became a pillar of strength for them, sharing his story and offering a listening ear.

In time, Ravi co-founded an organization focused on post-traumatic growth and resilience. The organization provided trauma-informed support to individuals affected by natural disasters, armed conflicts, and other life-altering events. Ravi's commitment to helping others find healing and hope became his life's purpose—a guiding light that emerged from the darkest depths of despair.

Post-Traumatic Growth Unleashed

Ravi's journey of post-traumatic growth was a testament to the resilience of the human spirit. Through introspection, self-compassion, and the support of his community, he not only survived the tragedy but also discovered a newfound sense of purpose and strength.

Ravi's organization flourished, impacting the lives of countless individuals and communities in need. His work reached far beyond the confines of Shantipur, touching hearts and inspiring resilience across the nation.

The story of Ravi's transformation is a testament to the potential for growth and renewal amidst the darkest of circumstances. Through the lens of post-traumatic growth, he found strength, purpose, and meaning in the face of unspeakable tragedy. Like a phoenix rising from the ashes, Ravi's journey reminds us that the human spirit is capable of transcending even the most devastating of events, and in doing so, discovering a resilience that can change lives. In the village of Shantipur, Ravi's legacy lives on—a beacon of hope for all who endure life's storms and seek the path of healing and growth.

"
WHEN HEARTS ALIGN AND SPIRITS ENTWINE,
RESILIENCE UNVEILS ITS EXTRAORDINARY GRACE,
ILLUMINATING THE PATH THROUGH LIFE'S TRIALS. **"**

8 Building Community Resilience

It takes me on an awe-inspiring journey through the heartlands of humanity, where the strength of togetherness becomes a force beyond measure. As I step into the heart of these vibrant communities, I witness the symphony of resilience, where every note is a testament to the power of unity. United by shared aspirations and unyielding determination, these communities transform crisis into opportunities, despair into hope, and adversity into triumph. Their stories resound with the harmonious rhythm of unwavering support, as hands join to lift each other from the depths of darkness.

Within these pages, I encounter the visionaries who embraced diversity and celebrated individuality, nurturing a culture of inclusion that radiates across generations. I walk beside the everyday heroes who championed social justice, breaking barriers and shattering stereotypes with their indomitable spirit. Their actions serve as beacons of inspiration, guiding us to create a world where every voice is heard, and every dream is nurtured.

Drawing upon the wisdom of ancient traditions and modern-day innovations, I explore how these communities cultivated a sanctuary of belonging. From bustling metropolises to quaint villages, I uncover the threads that connect hearts and minds, forging an unbreakable bond that shields against the storms of life. With courage as their compass, they navigate the uncertainties of the future, as one resilient entity, marching toward a brighter dawn.

This chapter celebrates the innate human capacity to thrive when we stand as one. It illuminates the ripple effect of compassion, as small acts of kindness cascade into a tidal wave of transformation. Through the intricacies of each story, I learn that a resilient community is not simply a product of time or place, but a testament to the extraordinary potential of the human spirit.

Join me on this odyssey of resilience, where unity knows no bounds and where the strength of a community can shape destinies and redefine humanity's trajectory. Together, we shall uncover the profound truth that resilience is not just an individual virtue; it is a collective force that ignites the soul of a community, forever inspiring the world with the limitless possibilities that arise when hearts beat as one.

Creating Supportive Environments

In the quest for resilience, we find that the human spirit is both shaped by and shapes its surroundings. The environments we inhabit play a pivotal role in nurturing our strength and fortitude, acting as crucibles where resilience is forged and tempered. Creating Supportive Environments is a chapter that delves deep into the transformative power of our surroundings, illuminating how the architecture of our lives can uplift us to conquer life's adversities.

The Built Environment: A mosaic of Resilience

In the heart of every city lies a mosaic of resilience, woven by the hands of architects and urban planners. The built environment, with its labyrinthine streets and towering structures, becomes a reflection of our collective aspirations. The design of physical spaces shapes human behaviour, influencing our interactions, and fostering a sense of community.

In bustling metropolises, where the rhythm of life is fast and relentless, architects strive to design spaces that provide respite and rejuvenation. Parks, gardens, and green spaces become sanctuaries amidst the concrete jungle, offering solace to weary souls seeking moments of tranquility. The symphony of urban life becomes harmonious when buildings and spaces align with the needs and dreams of its inhabitants.

From the towering skyscrapers of financial districts to the humble homes that dot the landscape, architecture becomes an embodiment of resilience. It stands as a testament to human ingenuity, transforming mere bricks and mortar into an ode to the human spirit's triumph over adversity.

Nature's Embrace: Healing and Harmony

Beyond the concrete jungles, we find solace in the embrace of nature's majesty. The serene whisper of the breeze through the trees and the vibrant hues of a sunset become the backdrop to life's journey. Nature's grandeur offers a balm to wounded souls, healing the scars of life's trials and tribulations.

Research reveals the profound impact of nature on mental well-being. Time spent in natural environments has been shown to reduce stress, anxiety, and depression, promoting a sense of connectedness with the world. The wilderness becomes a sanctuary where resilience is strengthened, and a sense of purpose is restored.

In rural settings, where life moves at a gentler pace, nature becomes an integral part of daily existence. Communities coexist harmoniously with the land, drawing sustenance and inspiration from its bounty. The resilience of rural life lies not only in the ability to weather external challenges but also in the bond forged with the land that sustains them.

Building Bonds: The Strength of Community

As we traverse the landscapes of resilience, we encounter the power of community in shaping supportive environments. A community is a tapestry of individuals, each thread woven together to create a vibrant whole. The strength of this collective lies in its ability to lift its members in times of need.

Communities that foster empathy and compassion thrive as reservoirs of resilience. In times of crisis, these bonds become lifelines, ensuring no one faces adversity alone. They create networks of support, empowering individuals to navigate life's storms with the knowledge that they are not alone in their struggles.

In diverse communities, we find the embodiment of unity amidst adversity. These melting pots of culture, language, and tradition become a celebration of the human spirit's capacity to adapt and thrive. They exemplify the resilience of unity, where a shared sense of purpose propels individuals to overcome even the most daunting challenges.

The Virtual rainbow: Connecting Hearts Across Distances

In the digital age, supportive environments extend beyond physical borders. The virtual realm becomes a bridge that spans continents, connecting hearts and minds across the globe. Through screens and keyboards, we find solace in the company of kindred spirits, forming communities that transcend geographical limitations.

The virtual world holds the power to provide a sense of belonging, especially to those who may feel isolated in their physical surroundings. It becomes a sanctuary where individuals can seek support, share their stories, and find inspiration in the triumphs of others.

However, the virtual realm also presents its challenges. As we navigate the complexities of online interactions, we must remain mindful of the impact our words and actions have on others. Creating supportive environments in the digital space calls for empathy, kindness, and understanding, fostering communities that uplift and empower.

A Symphony of Resilience: The Intersection of Environments

As we conclude our exploration of Creating Supportive Environments, we witness the beautiful symphony that emerges when physical, natural, and virtual environments converge. The built environment harmonizes with the surrounding nature, becoming a sanctuary for the human spirit. Communities grow and thrive amidst the nurturing embrace of their surroundings, fostering resilience that echoes through generations.

The world becomes an Interconnecte" tap'stry of resilience, where the spaces we inhabit and the connections we forge contribute to our collective strength. In each environment, we find a thread that weaves together the story of human endurance, an ode to the indomitable spirit that rises above life's turbulence.

As we move forward on this journey, let us continue to be architects of compassion, shaping environments that nurture and uplift. Let us embrace the lessons of Creating Supportive Environments and build a world where resilience flourishes in the hearts of all who inhabit it. The symphony of resilience awaits, and we are each instrumental in its composition.

Collective Healing and Empowerment

In the drapes of resilience, there exists a thread of collective healing and empowerment that weaves through the fabric of communities. It is the profound understanding that in supporting one another, we find strength, healing, and the power to rise above adversities. The journey of collective healing is one of vulnerability and compassion, where scars become stories and pain transforms into purpose.

Collective healing is the process through which communities come together to acknowledge and address their shared wounds, traumas, and challenges. It is a space where individuals can feel seen, heard, and understood, knowing that they are not alone in their struggles. In a world that can often feel disconnected, collective healing serves as a beacon of hope, reminding us of the power of human connection.

Empathy is the cornerstone of collective healing. It is the ability to step into someone else's shoes, to understand and share their feelings. In a world that can often feel isolating, empathy serves as a balm that nurtures wounded hearts and fosters unity.

Empowerment is the transformational force that drives collective healing to new heights. It is the belief that together, individuals can create positive change and shape their collective destinies. When communities empower their members, they give rise to a new generation of resilient individuals who are unafraid to confront challenges head-on.

In the drapes of resilience, each thread is woven with the power of collective healing and empowerment. It is a reminder that we are not solitary beings but interconnected souls, bound together by a shared human experience. Through empathy and empowerment, communities become sanctuaries of healing, nurturing spaces where wounds are transformed into wisdom and pain into purpose.

- In the small town of Serenity, nestled amidst lush green fields, a group of women gathers every week in a circle of solidarity. Here, they share their joys and sorrows, celebrating victories and comforting each other during difficult times. This circle has become a haven of collective healing, where the power of shared stories helps each woman find solace in knowing she is not alone.

- In the bustling metropolis of Metropolis, a community centre serves as a hub for collective healing. People from all walks of life come together to participate in storytelling sessions, workshops, and support groups. Through these interactions, they discover the strength that lies in vulnerability and the beauty of shared human experiences.

- In the town of Harmonyville, a group of young volunteers dedicates their time to visiting hospitals, nursing homes, and orphanages. Through simple acts of listening and offering a caring presence, they create a healing circle of empathy. The power of their compassion ripples through the community, leaving behind a trail of hope and connection.

- In the city of Unity, a community-driven initiative called "The Empathy Project" has transformed the lives of its residents. Through workshops and outreach programs, they have cultivated a culture of understanding and empathy. As conflicts arise, they turn to empathy as a tool for resolution, nurturing a community that stands strong in the face of adversity.

- In the rural village of Tranquillity, a group of women artisans has created a cooperative to uplift their community. Through their artistry and entrepreneurship, they have harnessed the power of collective empowerment to break free from cycles of poverty. Together, they have become a beacon of resilience, inspiring others to seize control of their destinies.

- In the heart of Metropolis, a community centre offers skill development programs and vocational training to at-risk youth. The centre empowers these young individuals, instilling in them a sense of self-worth and purpose. As they take charge of their lives, they become catalysts for positive change, transforming not only their futures but the fabric of their community.

Collective healing and empowerment extend beyond the boundaries of individual communities. They beckon society at large to address systemic challenges and work towards a more equitable and just world. When individuals unite for a common cause, the echoes of their actions reverberate far and wide.

In the city of Transformation, citizens have come together to tackle issues of homelessness and poverty. Through community-driven initiatives and advocacy, they have made significant strides in eradicating homelessness. Their resilience in the face of bureaucratic hurdles is an inspiration to communities worldwide, reminding us that collective healing is a potent force for social change.

In the town of Progression, a group of environmental activists has taken up the mantle of preserving the natural world. Through education, conservation efforts, and sustainable practices, they have become stewards of the environment. Their collective actions highlight the profound impact of individual efforts and ignite a movement for global change.

As we delve into the realm of collective healing and empowerment, we uncover the intricate shade of unity that binds communities together. Each thread, woven by the acts of compassion, empathy, and empowerment, creates a ripple effect that extends beyond boundaries.

From the smallest villages to the largest cities, the spirit of collective healing weaves its magic, transforming lives and shaping destinies. Through shared stories, empathy, and empowerment, communities rise above adversities, leaving a legacy of resilience for generations to come.

Mobilizing in Times of Crisis

In the fire of crisis, the human spirit reveals its true potential. It is a moment when communities unite, putting aside their differences to face adversity head-on. The ability to mobilize effectively in times of crisis is a hallmark of resilience, marking the difference between chaos and order, despair and hope.

Mobilization is the process of bringing people together, coordinating resources, and taking collective action in response to a crisis. It requires visionary leadership, clear communication, and a shared sense of purpose. In the face of chaos and uncertainty, mobilization becomes a beacon of light, guiding communities towards safety and stability.

The art of mobilization lies in fostering a sense of unity and common purpose. It is the realization that no challenge is insurmountable when people stand shoulder to shoulder, united by a common goal. In times of crisis, individuals tap into reservoirs of courage and determination, finding strength in their collective efforts.

The story of Unityville serves as a powerful example of effective mobilization in the face of crisis. When a devastating flood struck the town, the community came together to rescue stranded neighbours, provide shelter, and distribute essential supplies. Through the mobilization of volunteers and resources, Unityville weathered the storm with resilience and grace.

In the city of Harmony, an outbreak of a mysterious illness threatened to overwhelm the healthcare system. However, through swift mobilization, healthcare professionals, community leaders, and volunteers collaborated to set up testing centres, isolate infected individuals, and implement public health measures. Their united efforts saved countless lives and contained the outbreak.

In the aftermath of a powerful earthquake in Serenity, various organizations, governmental bodies, and community groups worked hand in hand to provide emergency aid, rebuild infrastructure, and support traumatized survivors. Their collective mobilization transformed devastation into an opportunity for renewal and growth.

Effective mobilization requires clear communication and coordination. In times of crisis, accurate and timely information can be a lifeline for communities. Leaders must ensure that information flows freely, empowering individuals to make informed decisions and take appropriate action.

The power of technology has revolutionized mobilization efforts. Social media platforms, community apps, and mass messaging systems enable swift communication and coordination. During a recent wildfire in Tranquillity, residents used social media to share real-time updates, organize evacuation efforts, and offer assistance to those in need.

Mobilization is not limited to physical actions; it extends to emotional and psychological support as well. In times of crisis, individuals may experience trauma, grief, and fear. Community mobilization includes creating safe spaces for emotional expression, providing counselling services, and offering mental health support.

Resilience is not solely about bouncing back; it is also about bouncing forward. Effective mobilization in times of crisis lays the groundwork for long-term recovery and growth. It involves strategic planning, resource allocation, and sustainable initiatives that empower communities to rebuild and flourish.

In the city of Progression, a devastating economic downturn threatened the livelihoods of thousands. Through mobilization efforts, local businesses collaborated to provide job training, employment opportunities, and financial support to those affected. The result was not only economic recovery but a stronger and more inclusive community.

In the town of Harmonyville, a community-led initiative focused on environmental conservation mobilized residents to adopt sustainable practices, reduce waste, and protect natural resources. Their collective efforts transformed Harmonyville into a model of eco-friendly living, inspiring neighbouring communities to follow suit.

During the pandemic, educational institutions in Metropolis swiftly mobilized to transition to online learning, ensuring continuity of education for students. The collaboration between educators, parents, and students showcased the power of collective action in times of crisis.

Effective mobilization requires inclusivity and representation. It is essential to recognize the unique needs and challenges faced by different segments of the community. Inclusive mobilization ensures that no one is left behind and that the most vulnerable members of society are adequately supported.

In the town of Serenity, community leaders mobilized to address the issue of food insecurity among low-income families. Through a collaborative effort, they established food banks, community gardens, and meal programs to ensure that everyone had access to nutritious food.

Resilient communities recognize that crises can serve as catalysts for positive change. The mobilization efforts during and after a crisis create opportunities to address underlying issues and systemic challenges. It is a chance to reimagine and rebuild a more equitable and sustainable future.

In the bustling city of Metropolis, a coalition of activists and policymakers mobilized to address urban inequality and homelessness. Their efforts led to the creation of affordable housing, job training programs, and support services for marginalized populations, making Metropolis a more inclusive and compassionate city.

Mobilization is not confined to large-scale crises; it is equally relevant in navigating personal challenges. When individuals face personal crises, mobilization involves seeking support from loved ones, reaching out to professional resources, and tapping into inner resilience.

The journey of mobilization is an ever-evolving one. As communities and individuals learn from each crisis, they become more adept at responding to future challenges. It is a process of continuous growth and adaptation, an affirmation of the human spirit's indomitable nature.

As we navigate the complexities of life, we are reminded that the power of collective mobilization lies within each of us. In times of crisis, our capacity for compassion, collaboration, and resilience shines brightest. When we stand together, we transform adversity into opportunity, chaos into harmony, and darkness into hope.

Rising from the Ashes

The Resilient Village of Utkarsh

In the quaint village of Utkarsh, nestled amidst the picturesque landscapes of rural India, lived a vibrant community bound by strong traditions and a deep sense of unity. The villagers had faced their fair share of challenges over the years, from harsh weather conditions to economic hardships, but their unwavering spirit and collective resilience had always seen them through.

Embracing Unity, Nurturing Strength

In Utkarsh, the spirit of unity was at the heart of the community's resilience. The village head, Rajan Bhai, was a wise and compassionate leader who believed in empowering every member of the community. Under his guidance, the villagers established a cohesive support network where each individual contributed according to their strengths. They organized regular meetings called "Sahyog Sabha" to discuss community challenges, celebrate their achievements, and make collective decisions. This sense of unity fortified their resilience and provided a strong foundation for growth.

Empowering through Education

Education was a key pillar of Utkarsh's resilience. Jyoti, a bright and determined young woman, had a vision to transform the village through education. With the support of Rajan Bhai and other villagers, she founded the "Utkarsh Vidyalaya," a school that aimed to provide quality education to all children, regardless of their socio-economic background. The school became a symbol of hope, nurturing young minds to dream big and overcome adversities with knowledge and skills.

Sustainable Development, Flourishing Future

Utkarsh faced the challenge of water scarcity, especially during the dry summer months. To address this, the village collectively initiated rainwater harvesting and water conservation practices. The village craftsmen, led by Vishal, designed innovative ways to capture rainwater, recharge groundwater, and utilize water efficiently. Their dedication and creativity in implementing sustainable practices not only solved the water crisis but also inspired neighbouring villages to adopt similar measures.

Strengthening Mental Health and Well-being

The emotional well-being of the community was paramount for their resilience. Deepika, a compassionate and skilled psychologist, recognized the need for mental health support in Utkarsh. With the help of Rajan Bhai and the villagers, she established the "Sahaj Samarpan" centre, a safe space for individuals to seek counselling and support during difficult times. The centre also organized workshops on meditation, yoga, and stress management, fostering a sense of peace and balance in the community.

Empowering Women, Transforming Lives

Utkarsh celebrated its women, acknowledging their immense contribution to the community's resilience. Rajani, a dynamic and ambitious young woman, founded the "Utkarsh Mahila Sangathan," a women's collective aimed at empowering women through skill development and income-generation programs. Through this initiative, women gained financial independence, enabling them to contribute actively to the community's growth and resilience.

Reviving Cultural Heritage, Preserving Identity

The village of Utkarsh took pride in its rich cultural heritage. Amar, a skilled artist and musician, led efforts to preserve and promote their traditional art forms, dance, and music. The villagers organized cultural festivals and events that showcased their talents and attracted visitors from far and wide. This cultural renaissance not only brought joy to the community but also provided economic opportunities, further strengthening their resilience.

Facing Natural Calamities with Courage

Utkarsh had experienced its fair share of natural calamities, including floods and cyclones. The village's resilience was tested during such times, and each instance became an opportunity for growth and learning. The villagers collaborated with government agencies, NGOs, and neighboring communities to develop disaster preparedness plans, emergency response teams, and evacuation protocols. Through these measures, Utkarsh was better equipped to face future challenges with courage and determination.

Fostering Inclusivity and Empathy

Utkarsh believed in embracing diversity and fostering inclusivity. The villagers welcomed migrant workers, offering them a sense of belonging and opportunities for livelihood. Ramesh, a compassionate elder, led efforts to bridge cultural gaps and ensure that every individual felt valued and respected. This spirit of inclusivity nurtured empathy within the community, creating a strong bond that transcended differences.

The story of Utkarsh is a testament to the power of collective resilience. By embracing unity, empowering through education, practicing sustainable development, nurturing mental well-being, empowering women, preserving culture, and fostering inclusivity, the villagers transformed their challenges into stepping stones towards a brighter future. Through the storms of life, they stood tall, sowing the seeds of resilience, and blooming with hope, strength, and harmony.

Utkarsh's journey serves as an inspiring example for communities worldwide, reminding us that when we come together with compassion, determination, and a shared vision, we can weather any storm and build a thriving future for generations to come. As we delve further into the essence of building community resilience, we discover the profound impact of collective efforts and the resilience that arises when we stand as one.

"
FAITH IS THE COMPASS THAT GUIDES YOU THROUGH
THE DARKEST STORMS, REVEALING THE STRENGTH AND
COURAGE WITHIN, LEADING TO SELF-DISCOVERY. "

9 Faith and Resilience

In the vast expanse of life's journey, there exists a profound force that can weather the most formidable storms and illuminate the darkest paths – that force is faith. Faith is not merely a belief in a higher power or divine providence; it is a profound trust in oneself, in the universe, and in the interconnectedness of all things. It is the unwavering conviction that, even in the face of adversity, there lies an opportunity for growth and transformation. This chapter delves into the intrinsic relationship between faith and resilience, showcasing how an unyielding belief can be the bedrock for discovering one's inner strength and navigating the complexities of life.

The Power of Belief

At the core of faith lies the power of unwavering belief – the profound knowing that everything happens for a reason and that every experience, whether pleasant or painful, carries a lesson. It is the understanding that setbacks are not dead-ends but stepping stones towards growth. Through captivating anecdotes and transformative narratives, we explore how individuals have harnessed the power of belief to transcend limitations, rise above challenges, and emerge stronger.

Finding Light in the Darkness

In the darkest of times, faith acts as a guiding beacon, leading individuals towards the light. This section unveils the stories of those who, amidst despair and sorrow, have discovered the strength to endure and the courage to hope. Their unwavering faith enabled them to find meaning in adversity, transforming their darkest moments into catalysts for personal growth and resilience.

The Journey Within

Faith is not merely an external force; it is an inward journey of self-discovery and transformation. In this section, we delve into the realms of self-exploration, showcasing how faith can act as a mirror, reflecting our true essence and untapped potential. It explores practices like meditation, prayer, and mindfulness that help individuals connect with their inner selves and uncover a reservoir of strength and resilience.

Embracing Uncertainty

Life is rife with uncertainties, and it is faith that allows us to embrace the unknown with grace and acceptance. This section shares stories of those who have faced adversity with equanimity and turned uncertainties into opportunities for self-growth and self-discovery. It provides insights into how faith can nurture a sense of surrender, enabling us to let go of control and find solace in the divine plan.

Cultivating Trust in Resilience

At the heart of faith lies a deep-rooted trust in the inherent resilience of the human spirit. This section sheds light on how individuals, guided by their faith, have weathered the storms of life with unwavering trust in their ability to bounce back. It explores the importance of building faith in one's capacity to rise, renew, and flourish in the face of challenges.

Building Faith Communities

Faith has the unique ability to unite people, fostering a sense of belonging and support. This section delves into the power of faith communities – spaces where individuals come together, share their struggles, and draw strength from one another. It explores the role of collective faith in creating resilient communities that uplift and inspire each other through life's trials.

The Transcendent Power of Hope

Hope, the harbinger of faith, is a transcendent force that carries individuals through the darkest nights. In this section, we unravel the profound relationship between hope and resilience, uncovering how hope can transform adversity into an opportunity for renewal and growth.

Embracing the Unseen

Faith invites us to embrace the unseen and the mystical, acknowledging that there is more to life than meets the eye. This section explores how individuals, driven by their faith, have discovered solace and purpose by connecting with something greater than themselves – whether it be nature, the universe, or the divine.

Rising from the Ashes

Like a phoenix rising from the ashes, faith empowers individuals to emerge stronger from the depths of despair. This section shares remarkable stories of resilience and transformation, highlighting how faith has helped individuals overcome seemingly insurmountable challenges, inspiring others to find hope in their darkest hours.

The Legacy of Faith

The impact of faith extends far beyond an individual's life, leaving behind a profound legacy. In this final section, we explore how the resilience born from faith has shaped individuals, families, and communities for generations, leaving a lasting imprint on the world.

In Chapter 9, we embark on a transformative journey, discovering the power of faith as a catalyst for resilience and self-discovery. Through inspirational stories and profound insights, we unlock the door to inner strength and unravel the profound mysteries that lie within us. As we navigate the chapters of our lives, may faith be the compass that guides us through the storms and illuminates our path towards personal growth and spiritual evolution.

Finding Strength in Spirituality

In the depths of human experience, there exists a sacred realm where the spirit finds solace and strength – the realm of spirituality. Beyond the confines of religious dogma, spirituality is an intimate connection with the transcendental, an awakening of the soul, and an exploration of the eternal truths that govern existence. It is a source of profound comfort and resilience, enabling individuals to find meaning and purpose in life's most challenging moments.

The Quest for Meaning

In the labyrinth of life's journey, the search for meaning is intrinsic to the human spirit. Spirituality serves as a guiding light in this quest, offering insights into life's deeper purpose and significance. It is through the contemplation of spiritual truths that individuals find a sense of belonging and purpose, grounding them amidst the chaos of the external world.

The Power of Prayer and Meditation

Prayer and meditation are ancient practices that bridge the gap between the finite and the infinite. They serve as pathways to attaining inner peace, quieting the mind, and transcending the limitations of the ego. Through captivating anecdotes, we explore how individuals have found solace and renewal through prayer and meditation, tapping into the wellspring of inner strength that resides within.

Cultivating Compassion and Forgiveness

At the heart of spirituality lies the profound virtues of compassion and forgiveness. When faced with adversity, cultivating compassion towards oneself and others can be a powerful tool for healing and resilience. This section delves into the transformative power of forgiveness, freeing individuals from the shackles of past pain and empowering them to embrace the present with an open heart.

Transcending Ego and Embracing Humility

The ego, with its relentless pursuit of validation and control, often becomes a hindrance to resilience. Spirituality offers a pathway to transcend the ego and embrace humility, empowering individuals to release the need for external approval and find strength in the depths of their true selves.

Surrendering to the Divine Plan

In the intricate tapestry of life, there are moments when one must surrender to the divine plan, trusting that the universe has a greater purpose in store. This section showcases how surrendering to the divine plan can be an act of liberation, liberating individuals from the burden of trying to control every aspect of their lives.

Drawing Inspiration from Sacred Texts and Teachings

Sacred texts and spiritual teachings have been a source of wisdom and guidance for countless generations. This section explores how individuals have found inspiration and resilience in the timeless truths and profound insights of spiritual scriptures and teachings.

The Healing Power of Rituals

Rituals and ceremonies have been an integral part of spiritual practices across cultures and civilizations. This section unravels how rituals can be transformative experiences, offering solace and healing to those navigating the storms of life.

Connecting with Nature and the Divine

Nature, with its awe-inspiring beauty and grandeur, has the power to evoke a sense of spiritual connectedness. This section delves into how individuals have found solace and resilience by immersing themselves in the wonders of the natural world, recognizing the divine presence in all living beings.

Awakening the Inner Light

Spirituality invites individuals to awaken the inner light that resides within – the spark of divinity that connects us all. Through introspective practices and soul-searching reflections, individuals can tap into this inner reservoir of strength and wisdom.

Living in the Present Moment

Spirituality reminds us of the importance of living in the present moment, for it is in the present that life unfolds. This section explores how being fully present can enhance resilience, enabling individuals to navigate challenges with grace and mindfulness.

We embark on a soul-stirring expedition into the realm of spirituality, discovering how it kindles the flame of resilience and ignites the spirit within. Through transformative practices, profound insights, and awe-inspiring revelations, we unlock the secrets of spiritual growth and self-discovery. As we traverse the sacred landscapes of our inner world, may spirituality be the compass that guides us towards profound resilience and profound inner peace.

Trusting the Journey

Life's journey is riddled with twists and turns, often veering off the well-trodden path into uncharted territories. In times of uncertainty and doubt, trusting the journey becomes an act of courage and resilience. This section explores the profound wisdom of surrendering to the flow of life, trusting that every step, even those obscured by darkness, holds a purpose and a lesson.

Embracing Uncertainty with Faith

Life is a tapestry woven with threads of uncertainty, and embracing it with unwavering faith is a testament to resilience. In this section, we delve into the transformative power of faith, exploring how it anchors us when confronted with the unknown and instils the confidence to navigate life's uncertainties.

Embracing Change and Letting Go

Change is the only constant in life, and yet, it can be one of the most challenging aspects to embrace. This section reveals how letting go of the past and embracing change is an act of courage, liberating individuals from the clutches of fear and propelling them towards new horizons.

Finding Strength in Surrender

Surrendering to the flow of life does not imply weakness; rather, it is a profound act of strength and trust. Through poignant narratives, we witness how individuals have found newfound strength in relinquishing control, allowing the currents of life to carry them towards unforeseen destinations.

The Transformative Power of Resilience

Resilience, when ignited by trust, becomes a force of transformation. This section illuminates how trust in the face of adversity can lead to profound growth, propelling individuals to transcend their limitations and emerge stronger than before.

Finding Meaning in the Journey

Within the labyrinth of life, finding meaning becomes a guiding star, leading us through the darkest nights. We delve into the stories of individuals who have found purpose and significance by trusting the journey, even when the destination remains shrouded in mystery.

Navigating Setbacks with Grace

Setbacks and challenges are inevitable, but it is our response that defines our resilience. This section uncovers how trusting the journey allows individuals to navigate setbacks with grace and dignity, transforming stumbling blocks into stepping stones on the path of growth.

Trusting Intuition and Inner Wisdom

Intuition is the voice of the soul, guiding us towards our deepest truths. This section explores how trusting our inner wisdom can be an anchor in the storm, leading us to make choices aligned with our higher purpose.

Forging Ahead with Determination

In the face of adversity, determination becomes a beacon of hope, inspiring individuals to forge ahead despite the odds. Through stories of indomitable spirits, we discover how trust in the journey fuels the flame of determination, lighting the way towards victory.

The Power of Resilient Hope

Hope is a reservoir of resilience that dwells within the human heart. This section illuminates how trusting the journey fosters a resilient hope, infusing individuals with the strength to endure even the darkest nights and emerge with newfound brightness.

In this quest we embark on a transformative journey of trusting the path laid before us, embracing the unknown with faith and resilience. In the tender embrace of trust, we unlock the gateways to profound growth, illuminating the path with each step, and unfurling the beauty of life's tapestry. Through the wisdom of trusting the journey, may we find solace in the midst of chaos, and may we dance with the rhythm of life, knowing that each twist and turn leads us closer to the essence of our being.

Resilience through Prayer and Meditation

In the hustle and bustle of modern life, where chaos and noise often drown out the whispers of the soul, finding solace in prayer and meditation becomes a sacred refuge for the resilient spirit. This section explores the transformative power of connecting with the divine, uncovering the profound impact of prayer and meditation on nurturing resilience and inner strength.

The Sanctity of Prayer

Prayer is a timeless practice that transcends cultures and religions, offering solace and guidance to seekers across the ages. In this section, we delve into the sacredness of prayer, exploring how it becomes a sanctuary for the soul, providing a profound sense of connection and comfort in times of trial.

Unveiling the Depths of Meditation

Meditation, a journey inward, is a gateway to self-discovery and clarity. This section delves into the multifaceted aspects of meditation, revealing how it can be a profound tool for building resilience, fostering mental fortitude, and finding a sense of tranquillity amidst life's storms.

Communing with the Divine

Beyond the realms of the material world lies the realm of the divine. Through heartfelt prayers and the art of meditation, individuals transcend the ordinary, communing with higher realms of consciousness. In this section, we explore the transformative power of such communion, witnessing how it bestows strength and resilience in the face of adversity.

The Healing Power of Faith

Faith is a gentle anchor that holds the human spirit steady when the tempest of life rages. This section shines a light on the healing power of faith, revealing how it nurtures resilience, fostering a profound belief in the inherent goodness of life.

Prayerful Gratitude

Gratitude is a tapestry woven from the threads of prayer and thankfulness. In this section, we uncover how cultivating a prayerful heart of gratitude can reframe life's challenges, birthing resilience from the most difficult circumstances.

Meditative Mindfulness: Embracing the Present

The present moment is a precious gift, often obscured by the worries of the past and anxieties of the future. Through the art of meditative mindfulness, individuals awaken to the beauty of the present, finding resilience in the serenity that dwells within the now.

Transcending Fear through Prayer

Fear can be a formidable foe on the journey of resilience. This section illuminates how prayer becomes a potent elixir, dissolving the shackles of fear, and empowering individuals to transcend limitations and step into the fullness of their being.

The Practice of Inner Stillness

Amidst the noise and chaos of the world, inner stillness becomes an oasis of peace. This section explores the practice of cultivating inner stillness through prayer and meditation, witnessing how it fosters resilience by centring individuals amidst life's ever-changing tides.

The Resilient Heart: Nurturing Compassion

In prayer and meditation, the heart expands, embracing all beings with compassion and love. This section unveils how cultivating a resilient heart of compassion becomes a source of strength, igniting a transformative ripple effect on the world.

Healing and Hope

In prayer and meditation, the threads of healing and hope weave a tapestry of resilience. This section delves into the transformative power of healing intentions, witness to the miracles born from the realm of the divine.

Transcending the Self: Prayer in Service

Prayer and meditation become a potent catalyst for transcending the limitations of the self, evoking a spirit of service towards others. In this section, we explore how prayer in service becomes an avenue for profound resilience, transforming both the giver and the receiver.

Harnessing the Power of Affirmations

Affirmations, like incantations of the soul, have the power to reshape reality. This section delves into the art of harnessing the power of affirmations through prayer and meditation, witnessing how they fortify resilience by instilling belief and unwavering confidence.

The Unseen Threads of Serendipity

In prayer and meditation, the soul dances in harmony with the universe, and serendipity weaves its unseen threads. This section reveals the synchronicities and magical moments that arise when resilience meets the divine flow.

Journeying Beyond Time and Space

Prayer and meditation become portals to realms beyond time and space, connecting individuals with the infinite. In this section, we glimpse the transcendence of time and the boundlessness of space, witnessing the resilient spirit touching the divine.

In the resplendent embrace of prayer and meditation, the heart opens to a universe of boundless possibilities. May the sacredness of these practices ignite a profound resilience within, illuminating the path of life with grace, serenity, and unwavering faith. In communion with the divine, may we find solace, strength, and the courage to rise above life's turbulence, embracing resilience as a sacred gift from the depths of our being.

The Mystic Resilience

Sadhguru Jaggi Vasudev's Extraordinary Journey

In the mystical land of India, amidst the enchanting Nilgiri Hills, lived a sage whose wisdom transcended time itself - Sadhguru Jaggi Vasudev. His magnetic presence and profound teachings had captivated millions worldwide, transforming lives and inspiring resilience in the face of life's challenges.

Born to a simple family in Mysore, young Jaggi was always inquisitive about the deeper meaning of life. Even as a child, he spent hours meditating under the ancient trees that surrounded his village. His innate connection with nature and an insatiable thirst for knowledge set the stage for his extraordinary journey.

As a teenager, Jaggi experienced a life-altering spiritual experience. Sitting on a large rock, he found himself transcending the limitations of his physical form, connecting with the very fabric of existence. This mystical encounter left an indelible mark on his soul, igniting a fire within him to seek higher truths.

Driven by an unyielding passion for inner exploration, Jaggi embarked on a pilgrimage across India, seeking guidance from various spiritual masters and gurus. His journey took him to the hallowed grounds of the Himalayas, where he delved into the depths of yogic practices and ancient wisdom.

Throughout his quest, Jaggi faced immense challenges and tests of his resilience. Adverse weather, treacherous terrains, and moments of doubt tested his determination. Yet, like a true yogi, he embraced each obstacle with equanimity, learning to find strength in surrendering to the flow of life.

As his spiritual insights deepened, Jaggi was drawn to the sacred Velliangiri Mountains in South India. There, under a tree, he experienced a profound state of meditation that would shape the course of his life forever. It was at this moment that he was initiated into the ancient yogic science by the yogi who had meditated under the same tree for over seven years.

With newfound wisdom, Jaggi returned to society, determined to share the transformative power of spiritual practices with the world. He founded the Isha Foundation, a non-profit organization dedicated to fostering global harmony and individual well-being.

Through Isha's various programs and initiatives, Sadhguru touched the lives of countless individuals, guiding them on the path of resilience and inner growth. His unique approach to spirituality, blending traditional wisdom with contemporary insights, resonated with people from all walks of life.

One of Sadhguru's most impactful initiatives was the Inner Engineering program, which aimed to equip individuals with powerful tools to manage their emotions and enhance their mental and emotional well-being. Through Inner Engineering, he empowered people to embrace life's challenges with grace and courage.

As Sadhguru's influence grew, so did his commitment to creating a positive impact on the world. The Rally for Rivers campaign, initiated by Isha Foundation, aimed to revive India's dying rivers by creating awareness about sustainable water management. His efforts garnered support from millions, spreading a message of environmental resilience.

In the face of adversity and criticism, Sadhguru remained steadfast in his mission to empower people with tools for inner transformation. He once said, "Resilience is not about enduring hardship; it is about transforming adversity into an opportunity for growth."

Sadhguru's teachings transcended borders, touching the lives of people worldwide. His spiritual discourses, infused with humor and wisdom, continue to inspire millions through online platforms, books, and global events.

As he embraced the title of "Mystic Resilience," Sadhguru's life became a living example of the profound impact spirituality could have on one's ability to navigate life's turbulent waters. His legacy remains a beacon of hope, guiding countless souls on the path of resilience and inner fulfillment.

In the sacred spaces of Isha Ashram, nestled amidst the Nilgiri Hills, Sadhguru continues to inspire seekers from all corners of the globe, reminding them that true resilience lies not in escaping life's trials but in embracing them with absolute grace and unshakable faith.

10 Resilient Growth

In the journey of human existence, resilience is the golden thread that weaves through the fabric of our lives, connecting moments of triumph and adversity. As we traverse the winding roads of challenges and uncertainties, resilience emerges as the steadfast companion, guiding us towards the promise of a brighter tomorrow. This chapter embarks on a journey of resilient growth, exploring the profound art of shaping a resilient mindset that embraces life's storms as catalysts for personal evolution.

The Phoenix Rising

Like the mythical phoenix that rises from its ashes, resilience empowers us to transcend the shadows of despair. In this section, we delve into the awe-inspiring stories of individuals who have emerged stronger, wiser, and more compassionate from the depths of adversity. Their tales of transformation inspire us to believe in the indomitable human spirit and its capacity to soar above life's challenges.

In the heart of darkness, we find the seeds of resilience taking root, and with every trial faced, the phoenix within us spreads its wings to greet the dawn of a new day. Through their journeys of profound growth, we witness the magic of resilience, igniting the fire of hope within us.

Cultivating a Growth Mindset

Within the fertile grounds of a growth mindset, resilience blossoms like a vibrant flower amidst the toughest terrain. This section explores the power of cultivating a mindset that views challenges as stepping stones on the path of personal evolution. By embracing the belief in our potential for growth and learning, we become architects of our destinies.

Drawing from the wisdom of philosophers, psychologists, and luminaries, we uncover the transformative power of a growth mindset that allows us to rewrite the narratives of our lives. By turning setbacks into opportunities, we pave the way for resilient growth, where every experience becomes a stepping stone towards greatness.

Embracing Change with Open Arms

In the grand symphony of life, change is the ever-present melody that accompanies our journey. Resilience lies not in resisting change but in embracing it with open arms. In this section, we navigate the art of gracefully adapting to life's twists and turns, finding strength in the face of uncertainty.

Through the stories of pioneers who have weathered the storms of change, we gain insights into the power of flexibility, resourcefulness, and resilience. As we dance with change instead of resisting it, we discover that life's uncertainties hold within them the seeds of growth and new possibilities.

The Healing Power of Forgiveness

The path to resilient growth is paved with the profound act of forgiveness. In this section, we explore the liberating power of forgiveness, both towards others and ourselves. By releasing the burden of grudges, we unshackle ourselves from the chains of the past, creating space for healing and renewal.

Through the inspiring tales of forgiveness from around the world, we witness the transformative alchemy that forgiveness brings. As we learn to extend compassion and understanding to those who have caused us pain, we free ourselves to embrace joy, peace, and wholeness.

Creating a Vision of Possibility

At the heart of resilient growth lies the ability to dream and envision a brighter future. In this section, we explore the art of creating a vision that ignites our passion and purpose, propelling us towards resilient growth.

By setting inspiring goals and crafting a vision that aligns with our deepest values, we become architects of our destinies. Through the lens of possibility, we reimagine what can be, opening doors to boundless potential and promising horizons.

Nurturing Self-Compassion

Within the embrace of self-compassion lies the crucible of resilient growth. This section delves into the profound impact of self-compassion on our ability to face challenges with courage and grace.

Through the wisdom of sages and modern-day thinkers, we learn to befriend ourselves, embracing imperfections and vulnerabilities with kindness. As we cultivate self-compassion, we nourish the roots of resilience, strengthening our ability to weather life's storms with fortitude and self-assurance.

Empowering Others Through Resilience

The path of resilient growth is not a solitary one but a collective endeavour that touches the lives of those around us. In this section, we explore the transformative power of empowering others through resilience.

Through acts of kindness, support, and empathy, we create a ripple effect of resilience that reverberates across communities. By offering a helping hand to those in need, we become catalysts for positive change, illuminating the path to a brighter future for all.

We stand at the precipice of boundless possibilities. The journey of resilient growth is one of self-discovery, courage, and transformation. We have delved into the intricate tapestry of resilience, learning to rise from adversity like the phoenix, embracing change with grace, and nurturing a vision of hope.

Through forgiveness and self-compassion, we have unlocked the gateways to healing, enabling us to write new chapters in our lives. Empowered by a growth mindset and inspired by the triumphs of others, we forge ahead on the path of resilient growth.

As we continue our quest to illuminate the way forward, may we be guided by the indomitable spirit of resilience, for it is in embracing life's storms that we forge a brighter future for ourselves and those we touch with our hearts and souls.

Setting Goals and Taking Action

In the grand tapestry of life, setting goals and taking decisive action is the thread that weaves dreams into reality. The power of resilience lies not only in weathering life's storms but also in steering our lives towards purposeful destinations. In this section, we embark on a journey of self-discovery, exploring the art of setting meaningful goals and aligning our actions with our deepest aspirations.

1. The Art of Visioneering

In the depths of our souls reside visions that stir our hearts and propel us forward. Visioneering is the art of crafting a compelling vision that ignites the spark of passion within us. By transcending the boundaries of the ordinary, we create visions that serve as beacons of hope, guiding us towards our desired future.

Drawing inspiration from visionary leaders and trailblazers, we unravel the secrets of visioneering. From vision boards to creative visualization, we learn how to manifest our dreams into reality, painting vibrant portraits of the lives we aspire to live.

2. Setting SMART Goals

In the realm of goal-setting, precision and clarity are the key to success. This section explores the concept of SMART goals - Specific, Measurable, Achievable, Relevant, and Time-bound. By transforming vague desires into well-defined objectives, we create roadmaps that lead us towards our dreams.

Through practical exercises and real-life examples, we learn how to set SMART goals that serve as stepping stones on the path to resilience and achievement. Armed with focus and determination, we navigate life's labyrinth with purpose and intention.

3. Embracing the Journey

As we embark on the pursuit of our goals, we encounter diverse landscapes and unexpected detours. Embracing the journey is the art of staying open to the lessons and opportunities that arise along the way. Resilience thrives when we adapt and grow in response to life's ever-changing landscape.

By cultivating an attitude of curiosity and flexibility, we turn detours into learning experiences and challenges into stepping stones. Through the tales of adventurers and explorers, we learn to savor the richness of the journey while keeping our eyes fixed on the horizon of our goals.

4. Overcoming Obstacles

In the pursuit of our dreams, obstacles are inevitable companions. This section delves into the essence of resilience - overcoming obstacles with courage and tenacity. When challenges arise, we summon the strength to face them head-on, knowing that each obstacle is an opportunity for growth. By embracing a problem-solving mindset and tapping into our innate resilience, we transform obstacles into stepping stones. Through real-life stories of perseverance, we witness the triumph of the human spirit over adversity, motivating us to press forward in the face of challenges.

5. Taking Inspired Action

To breathe life into our goals, we must take action that is fueled by inspiration and purpose. This section explores the art of taking intentional and inspired action towards our dreams. It is not merely about busy work but about aligning our actions with our values and aspirations. By fostering discipline and commitment, we create momentum that carries us closer to our dreams. Through the wisdom of achievers and change-makers, we uncover the keys to taking action that is fueled by passion, making the pursuit of our goals an exhilarating adventure.

6. Cultivating Patience and Resilience

In the world of goal-setting, patience is both a virtue and a necessity. This section delves into the art of cultivating patience and resilience as we navigate the twists and turns of our journeys. In moments of uncertainty and delay, resilience empowers us to stay the course with unwavering faith.

Through the tales of visionaries who faced setbacks and delays, we learn the art of staying patient while remaining steadfast in our pursuit. By nurturing resilience, we gain the strength to endure and emerge stronger on the other side of challenges.

In the symphony of resilience, setting goals and taking action is the harmonious interplay of vision and determination. As we explore the art of visioneering, SMART goal-setting, and embracing the journey, we equip ourselves with the tools to navigate the landscape of our dreams.

Through overcoming obstacles and taking inspired action, we march towards the realization of our aspirations, sustained by the cultivation of patience and resilience. As we tread this path of purpose and intention, may we find solace in the beauty of the journey and the fulfilment of our dreams.

Embracing Change and Uncertainty

In the ever-changing tapestry of life, change and uncertainty are constant companions. Like the ebb and flow of the tides, they shape our experiences, challenging us to adapt and evolve. Resilience beckons us to embrace the dynamic nature of existence and find strength amidst the winds of change and uncertainty.

In this section, we delve into the art of embracing change and uncertainty, uncovering the transformative power that lies within these seemingly daunting forces. Through wisdom gained from spiritual teachings, scientific insights, and real-life stories, we explore how embracing change can be a gateway to personal growth and resilience.

1. Navigating the Waters of Change

Change can sweep into our lives like a torrential storm, leaving us feeling ungrounded and vulnerable. In this chapter, we learn to navigate the waters of change with grace and fortitude. By recognizing that change is a natural part of life's rhythm, we release resistance and open ourselves to its transformative potential.

Drawing inspiration from the cycles of nature and the wisdom of ancient philosophies, we develop a mindset that embraces change as an ally rather than a foe. In times of upheaval, we find solace in knowing that within change lies the seeds of new beginnings and growth.

2. Embracing Uncertainty

Uncertainty can cast a shadow of doubt upon our lives, unsettling our sense of security and stability. This section explores the art of embracing uncertainty with an open heart and a curious mind. By letting go of the need for absolute certainty, we free ourselves to explore new possibilities and expand our horizons.

Through the lens of spiritual teachings and mindfulness practices, we learn to lean into uncertainty with trust and surrender. In the dance of uncertainty, we discover the resilience to face the unknown with courage, knowing that every moment is an invitation for growth and self-discovery.

3. Finding Opportunity in Change

Within the ever-shifting sands of change lies the treasure trove of opportunity. This chapter delves into the art of finding opportunity in the face of change. By reframing our perspective and embracing a growth mindset, we transform challenges into stepping stones towards our dreams.

Through real-life examples of individuals who harnessed change as a catalyst for success, we learn that resilience blooms when we seize opportunities presented by change. By developing the agility to adapt and innovate, we embark on a journey of continuous growth and transformation.

4. Embracing Impermanence

The impermanence of life can be both humbling and liberating. This section explores the profound wisdom of impermanence found in spiritual traditions and philosophical teachings. By acknowledging the transient nature of all things, we release attachment and embrace the beauty of the present moment.

Through practices of mindfulness and self-reflection, we cultivate an awareness of impermanence that infuses our lives with greater depth and meaning. In the acceptance of impermanence, we find the resilience to navigate life's changes with equanimity and a heart filled with gratitude.

5. Resilience in Times of Loss

Loss, a profound facet of the human experience, can leave us shattered and adrift. This chapter examines the resilience that arises from navigating the terrain of loss and grief. By honouring our emotions and embracing the healing power of compassion, we find strength in vulnerability.

Through stories of individuals who transcended loss and emerged with renewed purpose, we witness the indomitable spirit of resilience. By cultivating self-compassion and seeking support from our community, we find solace in knowing that in times of darkness, we are never alone.

6. The Dance of Change and Growth

In the grand symphony of resilience, change and growth dance together in harmonious rhythm. This final section explores the interplay between change and personal growth, revealing how they intertwine to shape our journey. By embracing change as a catalyst for growth, we embark on a transformative voyage of self-discovery and empowerment. Through the evolution of our thoughts, beliefs, and actions, we find ourselves resiliently anchored in the present, while reaching for the stars of our dreams.

In the grand symphony of life, embracing change and uncertainty becomes a graceful dance of resilience. As we navigate the waters of change and embrace the impermanence of existence, we find the courage to transform challenges into opportunities for growth.

Through the wisdom of spiritual teachings and the triumphs of human spirit, we realize that change is not to be feared but embraced as a potent force of transformation. With open hearts and minds, we step into the unknown with fortitude, knowing that within the embrace of change lies the seed of resilient growth and a brighter future.

Finding Purpose and Passion

Amidst the trials and triumphs of life, finding purpose and passion serves as a guiding compass, illuminating our path with clarity and fulfilment.

Resilience intertwines with purpose and passion, empowering us to navigate the labyrinth of existence with unwavering determination and a zest for life.

In this section, we explore the transformative journey of discovering purpose and igniting the flame of passion within. Through soul-searching reflections, inspiring anecdotes, and practical insights, we delve into the profound essence of living with purpose and embracing the things that set our souls on fire.

1. Unravelling the Tapestry of Purpose

Purpose, a tapestry woven into the fabric of our being, lies waiting to be unravelled. This chapter embarks on the soul-stirring quest of unearthing our unique purpose. By delving into our values, passions, and deepest desires, we uncover the threads that compose the intricate design of our life's purpose.

Through contemplative practices and stories of those who have found their calling, we awaken to the power of aligning our actions with purpose. In the pursuit of purpose, we embrace resilience as an anchor that keeps us steadfast amid life's tumultuous seas.

2. Passionate Pursuits: Fanning the Flames Within

Passion, an ember that smoulders in every heart, holds the key to unbridled joy and creative expression. This section explores the magic of igniting and nurturing our passions. By exploring our interests and dedicating time to activities that enliven our spirit, we stoke the flames of passion into roaring fires.

Through the journeys of passionate individuals who dared to pursue their dreams, we find inspiration to unleash our creative potential. In the pursuit of passion, we cultivate resilience as a shield against doubts and obstacles, trusting that our passion will propel us forward.

3. Aligning Purpose and Passion

When purpose and passion converge, a symphony of meaning and fulfilment resounds. This chapter delves into the powerful synergy of aligning purpose and passion. By recognizing the harmonious interplay between what drives us and what brings us joy, we unveil a sense of purpose that fuels our passions.

Through the stories of trailblazers who have merged their purpose and passion, we learn to embrace resilience as we embark on a journey guided by heart and soul. In the embrace of purpose and passion, we step into our unique calling with courage and resilience.

4. Embracing Change: Evolving Purpose and Passion

As life's tapestry unfolds, our purpose and passions may evolve, reflecting the ever-changing landscape of our inner world. This section explores the art of embracing change as our purpose and passions shift and transform. By releasing attachment to a fixed identity, we create space for growth and renewal.

Through stories of transformation and reinvention, we find inspiration to embrace resilience as we navigate the shifting tides of purpose and passion. In the dance of change and growth, we emerge as empowered beings, embracing the ebb and flow of life with grace.

5. Cultivating Resilience in Pursuit of Purpose

The pursuit of purpose can be a winding road, replete with challenges and obstacles. This chapter examines the role of resilience in navigating the path towards our purpose. By developing a resilient mindset and unwavering determination, we build the courage to overcome adversity.

Through the stories of individuals who persevered on their purposeful journey, we find solace in resilience as the anchor that keeps us steady amidst life's uncertainties. In the pursuit of purpose, we learn to view setbacks as stepping stones towards growth and transformation.

6. Passion as a Force of Resilience

Passion, a potent elixir that infuses life with vibrancy, becomes a force of resilience. This section explores the transformative power of passion in the face of challenges. By channelling our passion into purposeful action, we find the strength to overcome obstacles with unwavering determination.

Through stories of individuals who harnessed passion as a force of resilience, we learn to tap into the wellspring of our passions to fuel our journey towards purpose. In the embrace of passion as a resilience-building force, we awaken to the boundless potential within us.

In the interplay of purpose, passion, and resilience, we unearth the alchemy of a life lived with intention and joy. As we align our actions with purpose and fan the flames of passion, we traverse life's tapestry with grace and fortitude.

Through the wisdom of spiritual teachings and the triumphs of human spirit, we discover that purpose and passion are not static destinations but ever-evolving journeys. With hearts ignited by purpose and spirits fuelled by passion, we embrace resilience as our constant companion, propelling us forward towards a life of meaning, joy, and purposeful fulfilment.

Pinnacle of Perseverance

Indira Nooyi's Journey of Resilient Growth

In the annals of inspiring tales of resilience, one name stands tall – Indira Nooyi. Her journey from a small town in India to becoming one of the most influential business leaders in the world exemplifies the essence of Chapter 10: Resilient Growth: Forging a Brighter Future. Indira Nooyi's unwavering determination, strong sense of purpose, and passion for excellence are a beacon of hope for those seeking to overcome adversities and forge a brighter future.

1. Shaping Her Purpose: The Humble Beginnings

Indira Nooyi's story begins in Chennai, India, where she was born into a middle-class family. Raised with values of education and hard work, young Indira showed remarkable intellect and an unyielding spirit. Her purpose to make a difference in the world took root during her formative years, influenced by her mother's encouragement and the transformative power of education.

2. Passionate Pursuit of Excellence: From Chennai to the World

Fuelled by her passion for learning and a drive to excel, Indira pursued higher studies at the prestigious Indian Institute of Management Calcutta. Her exceptional leadership skills and strategic acumen led her to the United States, where she earned her Master's degree from Yale University.

3. The Journey Up the Corporate Ladder: A Tale of Resilience

Indira Nooyi's corporate journey was not without its challenges. As a woman of colour in the male-dominated world of business, she faced numerous hurdles. However, she defied expectations and proved her mettle, climbing the ranks at PepsiCo through sheer determination and resilience.

4. Embracing Change and Uncertainty: Pivoting to a New Vision

As CEO of PepsiCo, Indira navigated the ever-changing landscape of the global market. She recognized the importance of embracing change and uncertainty and encouraged a culture of innovation within the company. Her visionary approach led PepsiCo to diversify its product portfolio, including healthier options, in response to shifting consumer demands.

5. Purpose-Driven Leadership: Inspiring Positive Change

Indira Nooyi's leadership was rooted in purpose. She believed in responsible corporate citizenship and advocated for sustainable business practices and social initiatives. Under her guidance, PepsiCo implemented various environmental and social impact programs, leaving a lasting legacy of purpose-driven leadership.

6. Balancing Career and Family: The Power of Prioritization

Despite her demanding career, Indira Nooyi always prioritized her family and balanced her personal and professional life with grace. Her ability to juggle multiple responsibilities serves as a lesson in the importance of maintaining resilience and focus even in the face of challenging circumstances.

7. Crisis Management and Turning Adversity into Opportunity

Throughout her tenure as CEO, Indira Nooyi faced numerous challenges, including economic downturns and market fluctuations. Her adept crisis management skills and ability to turn adversity into opportunity demonstrated her unwavering resilience and strategic acumen.

8. Post-Traumatic Growth: A Journey of Learning and Adaptation

Indira Nooyi's resilience extended beyond corporate challenges. She embraced the concept of post-traumatic growth, utilizing setbacks as opportunities for learning and personal growth. Her philosophy of continuous improvement and adaptability remains an enduring source of inspiration for aspiring leaders.

Indira Nooyi's journey from a determined young girl in Chennai to a global business icon showcases the transformative power of resilience, purpose, and passion. Her life story exemplifies the essence of this chapter. Indira Nooyi's unwavering commitment to her purpose, her passion for excellence, and her ability to navigate challenges with unwavering resilience inspire us all to forge ahead with determination, embrace change, and build a brighter future. Her story serves as a proof to the indomitable human spirit and the potential that lies within each one of us to create a lasting impact on the world.

"
EVERY SETBACK IS A STEPPING STONE,
AND EVERY TRIUMPH A CELEBRATION OF THE
RESILIENCE WITHIN US. "

11 Celebrating Resilience

In the journey of life, we encounter numerous challenges and adversities. We navigate through the stormy seas, withstanding the tempests that threaten to drown us. Yet, in the face of turmoil, we find the remarkable human spirit that emerges stronger, wiser, and more resilient.

This chapter is a jubilant celebration of resilience - the indomitable spirit that thrives despite the odds. It is a testament to the human capacity to triumph over tribulations and emerge victorious. As we navigate the trials of existence, we realize that resilience is not merely a trait, but an art - a symphony of the soul, played with courage, fortitude, and grace.

Join me in this celebration of human spirit as we delve into stories of triumph, perseverance, and courage. Let's explore the myriad ways in which individuals have harnessed their resilience to overcome adversity and embrace life's challenges with unwavering hope. This chapter will not only inspire you but also remind you of the incredible power that lies within. It is a tribute to the resilience that resides within each of us - a force that transforms us from mere survivors to masters of our destinies.

Together, let us rejoice in the resounding victory of the human spirit and find inspiration in the tales of those who dared to dream, to rise, and to thrive in the face of life's most arduous tests.

As we start on this journey of celebration, let the stories within these pages ignite a fire within you - a fire that propels you forward, reminding you that you too possess the strength to rise above, to conquer, and to celebrate resilience.

Acknowledging Achievements

Embracing the Power of Triumph

In the story of life, achievements stand as vibrant threads, weaving together tales of determination, perseverance, and resilience. Each accomplishment, no matter how small, signifies a step taken towards progress, growth, and self-realization. The journey to success is often fraught with challenges, but it is in acknowledging these achievements that we unlock the true essence of resilience.

In this section, we celebrate the power of triumphs and the profound impact they have on our lives. It is a tribute to the moments of victory, both big and small, that shape our character and define our paths. As we delve into the stories of extraordinary individuals who have triumphed over adversity, we uncover invaluable lessons that serve as guiding lights on our own journeys.

Acknowledging achievements is not merely about basking in glory; it is about recognizing the dedication, hard work, and determination that went into realizing those dreams. It is about understanding that each triumph is a culmination of countless hours of effort, resilience, and unwavering faith in oneself.

At times, we may be hesitant to celebrate our achievements, fearing that it may come across as boastful or vain. However, embracing our triumphs is a powerful act of self-love and self-empowerment. It serves as a reminder of our potential and ignites the flame of possibility within us.

Through the stories of trailblazers who have achieved greatness against all odds, we learn that success is not an elusive dream; rather, it is a journey of resilience, fuelled by passion and purpose. It is a journey that demands us to embrace failure as a stepping stone and to persevere in the face of setbacks.

Each achievement is a testament to the strength of the human spirit, a beacon of hope for those facing their own struggles. It is a ripple that spreads far beyond the individual, inspiring generations to come. It is a testimony to the resilience that lies within each one of us.

In celebrating achievements, we not only honour the past but also pave the way for a future filled with boundless potential. It is a reminder that the road to success may be paved with obstacles, but with resilience as our compass, we can navigate the rough terrain with courage and grace.

As you read these inspiring stories of triumph, take a moment to reflect on your own journey. Acknowledge the milestones you have achieved, no matter how seemingly insignificant. Celebrate the growth, the progress, and the resilience that has brought you this far.

Remember, each achievement is a piece of the magnificent puzzle of life, contributing to the masterpiece that is your unique journey. Embrace the power of triumph and let it propel you forward as you continue to weave the tapestry of your extraordinary life.

Symphony of Resilience

In the bustling metropolis of Delhi and the cosmopolitan city of London, where dreams intermingled with the cacophony of life, lived two remarkable individuals - Riya and James. Separated by miles, yet bound by the tapestry of resilience, their journeys would converge in a symphony of hope and triumph.

Riya, a young woman hailing from a modest neighbourhood in Delhi, was passionate about classical dance. She found solace in the rhythmic sway of her body, weaving stories with each graceful movement. Despite facing societal pressures and financial constraints, Riya's spirit remained undaunted, and she pursued her art with unwavering dedication.

Across the globe, in the bustling streets of London, lived James, an aspiring musician with a love for the guitar. His melodies echoed through the city's bustling alleys, touching the hearts of passersby. Yet, the road to success was riddled with hurdles, and James found himself battling self-doubt and financial instability.

Both Riya and James harboured dreams of soaring to great heights in their respective fields, but life had different plans for them. A sudden tragedy struck Riya's family, forcing her to put her dreams on hold to support them. James, too, faced setbacks in his musical journey, struggling to find his place in the competitive world of the music industry.

Amidst the chaos and uncertainties, Riya and James found solace in faith and resilience. They drew strength from the unwavering support of their loved ones and the belief in their talents. Riya sought solace in the spiritual chants that echoed through the streets of Delhi, while James found inspiration in the bustling energy of London.

As destiny would have it, Riya's family's fortunes took an unexpected turn, allowing her to resume her passion for dance. She enrolled in a prestigious dance academy in London, a city known for its rich cultural tapestry. There, she met James, whose music had become a resounding voice in the city's artistic community.

The two kindred spirits found comfort in each other's journeys, understanding the struggles they had faced to pursue their dreams. In the city where dreams and realities intertwined, they formed an unbreakable bond, united by their unwavering faith in resilience.

Together, Riya and James embarked on a journey of growth and self-discovery. They took on every challenge with tenacity and grit, facing the highs and lows of artistic pursuits with unwavering determination. Their collaboration became a symphony of emotions, a fusion of classical dance and soulful music that touched the hearts of audiences worldwide.

Through their artistic endeavours, Riya and James inspired countless others to believe in the power of resilience. They held workshops in Delhi and London, sharing their stories of triumph over adversity, igniting sparks of hope in the hearts of budding artists.

Their journey of resilience took them to grand stages and prestigious platforms, where they celebrated the rich cultural heritage of both Delhi and London. They became ambassadors of hope, proving that no matter where life takes you, faith in one's dreams and the strength to endure could lead to an extraordinary symphony of resilience.

As Riya's dance embraced the vibrant colours of Delhi and James's music resonated with the pulsating energy of London, they crafted a narrative that transcended geographical boundaries. They showed the world that the tapestry of resilience could be woven from the threads of faith, passion, and unwavering determination.

In the bustling metropolis of Delhi and the cosmopolitan city of London, Riya and James became a living testament to the transformative power of resilience. Their story proved that no matter the odds, dreams could find a way to take flight, soaring above the challenges of life, and creating a symphony that would resonate for generations to come.

Title

Embracing Resilient Role Models

Triumph in the Face of Adversity

In this section, we explore the lives of three remarkable individuals who have risen above life's challenges and become beacons of hope and inspiration. These role models exemplify the true spirit of resilience, showcasing that adversity can be a stepping stone to greatness. Their stories serve as a reminder that no obstacle is insurmountable, and with determination and fortitude, one can achieve the extraordinary.

1. The Unwavering Determination of Malala Yousafzai

Malala Yousafzai's story is one of courage, determination, and a relentless pursuit of education in the face of adversity. Born in the Swat Valley of Pakistan, Malala faced numerous challenges in her quest for education, particularly as a girl in a society where girls' education was discouraged. Despite facing threats from the Taliban, she continued to speak out for the right to education and women's rights.

In 2012, at the age of 15, Malala was targeted in an assassination attempt by the Taliban. She was shot in the head while returning from school. However, this traumatic experience only fueled her passion for advocacy. Malala not only survived but emerged stronger and more resolute in her mission.

Today, Malala is a global advocate for girls' education and women's rights, and her resilience has earned her the Nobel Peace Prize. She founded the Malala Fund, an organization that works to ensure every girl receives 12 years of free, safe, and quality education. Malala's unwavering determination and fearlessness in the face of adversity have made her an international role model, inspiring millions to fight for their right to education.

2. The Indomitable Spirit of Nick Vujicic

Born without arms and legs, Nick Vujicic's journey has been one of embracing challenges with an indomitable spirit. Despite facing physical limitations, Nick refused to let his circumstances define him. He learned to do everyday tasks using his feet and even became skilled at swimming, surfing, and playing golf. More importantly, he developed an unshakable positive outlook on life.

Nick faced bullying and struggled with feelings of hopelessness in his teenage years. However, he eventually found his purpose and passion in motivational speaking. He began sharing his story of triumph over adversity and the power of embracing one's uniqueness. Through his organization, Life Without Limbs, Nick spreads messages of hope, love, and resilience to people around the world.

His resilience and unwavering faith have inspired countless individuals to overcome their challenges and find the strength to pursue their dreams. Nick's story is a testament to the human spirit's ability to rise above difficulties and find joy and purpose in the face of adversity.

3. The Enduring Grit of Oprah Winfrey

Oprah Winfrey's journey from a challenging childhood to becoming one of the most influential women in the world is a tale of enduring grit and determination. Born into poverty in rural Mississippi, Oprah faced numerous hardships, including abuse and discrimination. Despite these adversities, she remained steadfast in her pursuit of education and a better life.

In her early career, Oprah encountered setbacks and challenges. However, she refused to be defined by her circumstances and used her struggles as stepping stones to success. Her talk show, "The Oprah Winfrey Show," became a platform for empowering discussions and inspiring stories, making it one of the most-watched television programs in history.

Through her media empire and philanthropic endeavours, Oprah has become an icon of resilience and empowerment. She has used her platform to uplift others, advocating for education, women's rights, and social justice.

The lives of Malala Yousafzai, Nick Vujicic, and Oprah Winfrey are testament to the power of resilience. Each faced unique challenges and adversities, but they never allowed their circumstances to define them. Instead, they harnessed their inner strength to overcome obstacles, inspire change, and create a lasting impact on the world.

Their stories remind us that resilience is not just about bouncing back from adversity; it's about thriving despite it. These role models teach us that with unwavering determination, a positive mindset, and a willingness to embrace challenges, we can forge our path to a brighter future. Their journeys inspire us to embrace our own resilience and believe in the power of the human spirit to triumph over any adversity.

Embracing the resilience of these role models in our own lives can be a powerful source of inspiration and motivation. Here are some ways we can incorporate their teachings and experiences into our daily lives:

1. Learn from Their Mindset: One of the key factors that set these role models apart is their positive and determined mindset. We can adopt a similar outlook by focusing on gratitude, optimism, and self-belief. Cultivate a growth mindset that sees challenges as opportunities for growth and learning.

2. Pursue Our Passions: These role models pursued their passions with unwavering dedication. Identify your passions and interests and take steps towards realizing your goals. Embrace your uniqueness and let it guide you towards a fulfilling life.

3. Advocate for Change: Each of these role models made a difference by advocating for important causes. Find issues that resonate with you and get involved in social or community initiatives. Small actions can create significant change.

4. Overcome Adversity: The journeys of these role models are a testament to the human spirit's ability to overcome adversity. When facing challenges, draw strength from their experiences and remember that resilience is within each of us.

5. Seek Support and Inspiration: Surround yourself with a supportive network of friends, family, or like-minded individuals who uplift and inspire you. Engage with motivational content, books, or podcasts that share stories of resilience and triumph.

6. Practice Self-Reflection: Take time to reflect on your own life, values, and goals. Use these role models' experiences as a guide to align your actions and decisions with your purpose and vision.

7. Be Persistent: Resilience often involves persistence and determination. When faced with setbacks, remember that success is built on continuous effort and perseverance.

8. Learn from Setbacks: Instead of being discouraged by failures, view them as opportunities to learn and grow. Embrace the lessons from setbacks and use them to fuel your determination.

9. Spread Positivity: Like these role models, use your platform and voice to spread positivity and inspire others. Your words and actions can have a ripple effect, touching the lives of those around you.

10. Focus on Personal Growth: Embrace a journey of continuous growth and self-improvement. Set meaningful goals and take deliberate steps to develop your skills and talents.

By incorporating these practices into our lives, we can cultivate resilience and embrace the transformative power of these inspiring role models. Their stories remind us that we too have the strength to rise above challenges and forge a brighter future.

Cultivating Gratitude

The Resilient Pathway to Happiness and Fulfilment

In a world often filled with hustle and bustle, stress, and challenges, it can be easy to lose sight of the simple joys and blessings that surround us. Gratitude, the practice of acknowledging and appreciating the goodness in our lives, holds the power to transform our perspective, enhance our well-being, and build resilience.

In this chapter, we explore the profound impact of cultivating gratitude in our lives. We delve into the science behind this practice, understanding how it rewires our brains, strengthens our relationships, and fuels our resilience. From the streets of Delhi to the bustling lanes of London, people from all walks of life have embraced gratitude and experienced its transformative effects.

The Science of Gratitude

Before we dive into the practical aspects of cultivating gratitude, it's essential to understand the science behind this practice. Research in positive psychology has shown that gratitude is more than just a fleeting emotion; it is a mindset that can be nurtured and developed over time.

When we express gratitude, our brains release neurotransmitters such as dopamine and serotonin, which are responsible for feelings of pleasure and contentment. This not only makes us feel good in the moment but also rewires our brains to be more attuned to positive experiences in the future.

Moreover, gratitude activates the brain's prefrontal cortex, the region responsible for decision-making and emotional regulation. This enhanced cognitive control enables us to better navigate through challenges and make sound choices.

Gratitude also impacts our physical health. Studies have revealed that individuals who practice gratitude regularly experience lower levels of stress, improved sleep quality, and enhanced immune function. Such physical well-being further bolsters our resilience to face life's adversities.

The Practice of Gratitude

The beauty of cultivating gratitude lies in its simplicity. It doesn't require grand gestures or material possessions. Instead, it begins with a mindful awareness of the blessings present in each moment.

1. Gratitude Journaling: A popular and effective way to practice gratitude is through journaling. Each day, take a few moments to jot down things you are grateful for. It could be as simple as the warmth of the morning sun, a smile from a loved one, or a delicious meal shared with friends.

2. Counting Blessings: Whenever you find yourself feeling overwhelmed or stressed, pause, and make a mental note of three things you are grateful for. This simple act can instantly shift your focus from what's lacking to what's abundant in your life.

3. Gratitude Letters: Expressing gratitude to others can deepen your connections and strengthen your relationships. Take the time to write a heartfelt letter to someone who has positively impacted your life and share how much their presence means to you.

4. Mindful Gratitude: During moments of mindfulness or meditation, intentionally reflect on the blessings in your life. Allow yourself to bask in the feelings of gratitude and let them permeate your being.

5. Gratitude Walks: Take a leisurely stroll in nature and use this time to appreciate the beauty of your surroundings. Observe the colors, textures, and sounds of the environment, and acknowledge the wonder of the natural world.

6. Gratitude Rituals: Create meaningful gratitude rituals that fit your lifestyle. It could be saying a thank-you prayer before meals, creating a gratitude jar to fill with notes of appreciation, or sharing a daily gratitude moment with your family.

The Transformative Power of Gratitude

As we incorporate gratitude into our daily lives, we begin to experience profound transformations in our inner and outer worlds.

1. Shift in Perspective: Gratitude allows us to reframe challenges as opportunities for growth and learning. Rather than viewing obstacles as roadblocks, we see them as stepping stones on our path to resilience and self-discovery.

2. Enhanced Relationships: Expressing gratitude deepens our connections with others. When we acknowledge and appreciate the contributions of our loved ones, it fosters trust, strengthens bonds, and creates a positive cycle of giving and receiving.

3. Resilient Mindset: Gratitude nurtures a resilient mindset, enabling us to bounce back from setbacks with grace and determination. It reminds us of the abundance of resources and support available to us, instilling confidence in our ability to overcome challenges.

4. Attitude of Abundance: By focusing on what we have rather than what we lack, we develop an attitude of abundance. This abundance mindset opens us up to new opportunities and experiences, inviting more positivity into our lives.

5. Gratitude in Adversity: When faced with adversity, gratitude becomes an anchor of stability. It empowers us to find silver linings in difficult situations, fostering hope and optimism even in the darkest of times.

Gratitude Stories from Delhi to London

In Delhi, amidst the bustling streets and vibrant culture, lies the story of Aisha, a young woman who discovered the power of gratitude amidst personal struggles. Aisha, a recent college graduate, faced the challenge of finding a job in a highly competitive market. Frustration and self-doubt crept into her mind, clouding her outlook.

In the midst of her struggles, Aisha stumbled upon a gratitude journaling practice. Each evening, she reflected on the small victories and blessings of the day, acknowledging the support of her family, the encouraging words of a friend, and the beauty of a blooming flower on her walk home. Slowly, her perspective shifted, and she began to approach job interviews with a newfound sense of confidence and optimism.

With the weight of self-doubt lifted, Aisha secured a job at a prestigious company, attributing her success to the transformative power of gratitude. She continues to practice gratitude daily, savoring the joys and navigating the challenges of life with resilience.

Meanwhile, in the bustling city of London, Rohan, a successful entrepreneur, embodies gratitude as a cornerstone of his leadership. Rohan built his business from the ground up, overcoming numerous hurdles along the way. Despite his achievements, he remains grounded and humble, regularly expressing gratitude to his team for their hard work and dedication.

Rohan's gratitude has created a culture of appreciation within his organization. Employees feel valued and inspired to give their best, fostering a sense of unity and camaraderie. In turn, the company's success has grown, and it continues to make a positive impact in the lives of its customers and the community.

The Gratitude Ripple Effect

As Aisha and Rohan discovered, gratitude is a potent force that ripples through our lives and the lives of those around us. When we embrace this practice, we tap into the wellspring of resilience within us and find strength in the face of adversity.

From the vibrant streets of Delhi to the bustling lanes of London, the power of gratitude knows no bounds. It is a universal language that unites us, transcending cultures and borders. As we continue our journey of resilience, let us carry the torch of gratitude with us, illuminating our path and inspiring others to embrace the transformative power of gratitude.

" SUCCESS IS NOT FINAL, FAILURE IS NOT FATAL:
IT IS THE COURAGE TO CONTINUE THAT COUNTS. "

12 Resilience in Professional Pursuits

Welcome to Chapter 12: Resilience in Professional Pursuits - an inspiring and transformative journey that delves deep into the realm of resilience intertwined with the pursuit of success. As we embark on this captivating exploration, we uncover the profound connection between resilience and self-discovery, and how they converge to propel us towards unparalleled achievements.

Navigating the Turbulent Seas of Success

Professional pursuits often lead us through turbulent seas, but resilience becomes our steadfast anchor, allowing us to weather the storms and emerge stronger than ever. It empowers us to navigate through challenges with grace and determination, embracing setbacks as stepping stones towards greater heights.

Unleashing the Power Within

Resilience is the key that unlocks the dormant potential within us. It empowers us to dig deep and discover the wellsprings of strength and courage that lie within. With resilience as our ally, we break through barriers, unleashing the power to manifest our wildest dreams.

From Adversity to Achievement

With resilience as our guide, we transform adversity into a launching pad for achievement. It is in the face of challenges that we discover our true capabilities and unearth the well of creativity that propels us towards greatness.

Adaptability: The Key to Thriving

In the ever-changing landscape of professional life, adaptability is the currency of success. Resilience teaches us to embrace change with an open heart, recognizing that flexibility and innovation are the keys to thriving in any circumstance.

Discovering Purpose and Passion

Resilience leads us on a profound journey of self-discovery, uncovering our purpose and igniting the flames of passion within us. As we align our professional pursuits with our deepest values and desires, we find meaning and fulfilment in every endeavour.

Mastery Through Mindset

The resilient mind is a fertile ground for growth and mastery. It enables us to cultivate a growth mindset, seeing every challenge as an opportunity for learning and improvement. With resilience, we shift from a fear of failure to an excitement for growth.

The Path of Fearless Leadership

Resilience transforms us into fearless leaders, guiding and inspiring those around us through turbulent waters. It is the beacon of hope that drives us to lead by example, empowering our team to rise above challenges and reach new heights of success.

Embracing the Art of Balance

As we chase our professional aspirations, resilience reminds us of the importance of balance. It guides us to nurture our well-being and maintain harmonious relationships, recognizing that true success lies in the alignment of mind, body, and soul.

Living with Gratitude

In the pursuit of success, resilience encourages us to pause and embrace gratitude. It is through appreciation and thankfulness that we attract abundance, creating a positive ripple effect that enhances our professional journey.

A Symphony of Growth

The journey of resilience is a symphony of growth—an ever-evolving melody that harmonizes with our deepest aspirations. It is the unwavering belief in our potential that fuels our passions, igniting the fire that drives us towards excellence.

Resilience in Professional Pursuits is an awe-inspiring voyage that celebrates the unyielding spirit of resilience and its profound impact on our pursuit of success. Through resilience, we embrace challenges with confidence and transform setbacks into stepping stones. It is the secret sauce that propels us towards our true potential, unveiling the path to unprecedented achievement. As we embrace resilience and the power of self-discovery, we step into our role as fearless leaders, forging a brighter and more fulfilling future in our professional endeavours.

Overcoming Career Challenges

Every professional journey is laden with obstacles and uncertainties, but it is the resilient spirit that empowers us to rise above adversities and reach new heights of success. In this chapter, we explore the transformative power of resilience in navigating the rough waters of the corporate world and overcoming career hurdles with grace and determination.

Understanding Career Challenges

Career challenges come in various shapes and sizes—unexpected job loss, tough competition, workplace conflicts, or a shift in industry trends. These hurdles often test our mettle and challenge our confidence, leaving us uncertain about our capabilities. However, it is essential to recognize that career challenges are not synonymous with failure; rather, they present unique opportunities for growth and self-improvement.

Resilience: The Steadfast Anchor

At the core of overcoming career challenges lies resilience—a quality that fortifies our resolve and enables us to stay afloat amidst turbulent times. Resilience equips us with the ability to adapt to changing circumstances, bounce back from setbacks, and cultivate a growth mindset that views challenges as stepping stones rather than stumbling blocks.

A Relevant Example: The Phoenix Rises

Consider the journey of Riya, a bright and ambitious marketing professional. After years of hard work, Riya landed her dream job as a marketing manager in a prominent multinational company. Excited and full of aspirations, she embraced her role with enthusiasm and dedication. However, as time passed, Riya encountered unforeseen challenges—declining market demand, increasing competition, and evolving consumer preferences. The pressure of meeting demanding targets and keeping up with changing industry trends began taking a toll on her confidence.

Facing Redundancy

One day, the unexpected happened—Riya was informed that her position was being made redundant due to company restructuring. Shocked and disheartened, she felt a sense of failure creeping in. The fear of uncertainty and the thought of starting afresh in a new organization weighed heavily on her.

Embracing Resilience

Despite the initial shock, Riya decided to embrace resilience as her guiding light. Instead of succumbing to self-doubt, she acknowledged her feelings and embraced the opportunity to learn and grow. Riya realized that her value as a professional extended beyond her job title and that she possessed a unique set of skills that could transcend any position.

Discovering a New Direction

With resilience as her anchor, Riya embarked on a journey of self-discovery. She explored her passions and considered avenues that aligned with her interests and expertise. During this introspective phase, she stumbled upon an emerging field in digital marketing—an area where she could leverage her creativity and strategic thinking.

Pursuing Growth and Upskilling

Riya realized that her professional journey had taken a detour, but she saw it as a chance to reinvent herself. With unwavering resilience, she enrolled in courses to upskill herself in digital marketing, attending workshops, and gaining hands-on experience. Riya's eagerness to adapt and evolve impressed prospective employers and colleagues alike.

Seizing the Opportunity

As she honed her skills, an exciting opportunity presented itself—a startup seeking a marketing head with expertise in digital marketing. Riya saw this as a chance to make her mark in a dynamic and growing company. Drawing upon her resilience and newfound knowledge, she aced the interviews and secured the position.

Riya's career challenges had transformed her into a stronger, more adaptable professional. With resilience, she had risen like a phoenix from the ashes of uncertainty, forging a new and promising path. Today, she is not only a respected marketing head but also a source of inspiration for her team, encouraging them to embrace resilience and fearlessly tackle challenges.

The story of Riya exemplifies the power of resilience in overcoming career challenges. In the face of adversity, resilience is the unwavering force that propels us forward, empowering us to navigate uncertainty, reinvent ourselves, and emerge triumphant. By cultivating resilience, we not only overcome career hurdles but also discover our true potential and capacity for growth. Embrace resilience as your guiding light, and like Riya, you too can rise above the waves of career challenges, forging a fulfilling and successful path in the professional world.

Building a Resilient Workforce

Nurturing a Thriving Team

It wouldn't be complete without exploring the importance of building a resilient workforce. In today's fast-paced and ever-changing business landscape, organizations need employees who can weather storms and adapt to challenges with ease. A resilient workforce is not just the backbone of an organization; it is the driving force that propels growth and success.

Understanding a Resilient Workforce

A resilient workforce comprises individuals who possess the ability to bounce back from setbacks, embrace change, and maintain a positive attitude in the face of adversity. These employees are not only better equipped to handle stressful situations but also display higher levels of productivity, engagement, and loyalty. A resilient workforce fosters an environment of collaboration, innovation, and adaptability, paving the way for long-term success.

Nurturing Resilience in the Workplace

Creating a resilient workforce requires a concerted effort from leaders and organizations. It involves fostering a culture that prioritizes employee well-being, encourages continuous learning, and provides ample opportunities for growth and development. It also requires acknowledging and addressing the challenges employees face, promoting open communication, and providing support during difficult times.

A Strong Example

The Company that Rose Above the Pandemic

Consider the case of Stellar Solutions, a mid-sized IT company based in Bengaluru, India. Like many other organizations, Stellar Solutions faced immense challenges during the COVID-19 pandemic. The sudden shift to remote work, economic uncertainties, and heightened anxiety among employees posed significant obstacles.

Embracing Empathy and Flexibility

In the face of these challenges, the leadership at Stellar Solutions demonstrated exceptional empathy and flexibility. They recognized the unique circumstances employees were dealing with and introduced flexible working hours to accommodate individual needs. They also encouraged open communication and actively listened to the concerns and suggestions of their team members.

Providing Skill Development Opportunities

To keep their workforce engaged and motivated, Stellar Solutions invested in skill development programs and online workshops. They encouraged employees to learn new skills, adapt to the virtual work environment, and enhance their technical expertise. This not only boosted employee morale but also equipped the workforce to tackle new projects and client demands.

Promoting Work-Life Balance

Understanding the importance of work-life balance during challenging times, Stellar Solutions introduced initiatives to promote employee well-being. They organized virtual wellness sessions, yoga classes, and mental health awareness programs. The company also provided regular breaks and encouraged employees to take time off to recharge and rejuvenate.

Recognizing and Celebrating Achievements

In times of uncertainty, recognizing and celebrating even small achievements can have a profound impact on employee morale. Stellar Solutions adopted a practice of acknowledging and appreciating the efforts of their employees through virtual recognition ceremonies and monthly accolades. This not only fostered a sense of belonging but also reinforced a positive work culture.

The Triumph

Thanks to the resilience of its workforce and the supportive environment created by the organization, Stellar Solutions navigated the pandemic successfully. They adapted to remote work seamlessly, won new clients, and even expanded their services to cater to emerging market demands. The company's strong foundation of resilience propelled them to greater heights, even in the face of unprecedented challenges.

Building a resilient workforce is the cornerstone of any thriving organization. By nurturing a culture of empathy, flexibility, and continuous learning, leaders can inspire their employees to face challenges head-on and embrace change with confidence. The story of Stellar Solutions illustrates the transformative power of resilience in driving success and growth. When organizations prioritize the well-being and growth of their employees, they sow the seeds for a workforce that can weather any storm and emerge stronger than ever before. In building a resilient workforce, organizations not only secure their future but also create a workplace that empowers individuals to excel and thrive in their professional journey.

Leadership and Resilience

Guiding the Path to Success

In the realm of business, leadership plays a pivotal role in steering organizations through turbulent waters and inspiring their teams to overcome challenges. Resilient leaders possess the unique ability to navigate uncertainty with grace, maintain a sense of purpose, and empower their teams to thrive in the face of adversity. In this chapter, we will explore the essential traits of resilient leaders and delve into a powerful framework that can guide leaders in fostering resilience within their organizations.

The Traits of Resilient Leaders

1. Vision and Purpose: Resilient leaders have a clear vision and purpose that anchors them during difficult times. They articulate a compelling vision for the future and communicate it effectively to their teams, instilling a sense of direction and meaning in their work.

2. Emotional Intelligence: Emotional intelligence is a cornerstone of resilience in leadership. Resilient leaders understand their own emotions and can empathize with the feelings and experiences of their team members. This enables them to build strong connections and trust within their teams.

3. Adaptability and Flexibility: In a constantly changing world, resilient leaders are adaptable and flexible. They embrace change as an opportunity for growth, rather than a threat, and can pivot their strategies and plans when needed.

4. Decision-Making Under Pressure: Resilient leaders can make sound decisions even in high-pressure situations. They remain calm and composed, relying on data and insights to guide their choices and avoid reactive decision-making.

5. Self-Awareness: Resilient leaders have a deep understanding of their strengths and weaknesses. They continuously seek self-improvement and are open to feedback, recognizing that personal growth is essential for effective leadership.

The Resilient Leadership Framework

The Resilient Leadership Framework provides a structured approach for leaders to cultivate resilience within themselves and their teams. This framework is built on the foundation of self-awareness, emotional intelligence, and a growth mindset.

1. Cultivate Self-Awareness

Resilient leaders begin by cultivating self-awareness. They take the time to reflect on their values, strengths, and areas of growth. They identify their triggers and stressors, recognizing how these factors can impact their decision-making and leadership style.

2. Foster Emotional Intelligence

Next, resilient leaders focus on fostering emotional intelligence within themselves and their teams. They actively listen to their team members, empathize with their challenges, and provide support when needed. They create a psychologically safe environment where team members feel comfortable expressing their thoughts and emotions.

3. Develop a Growth Mindset

Resilient leaders embrace a growth mindset, seeing challenges and failures as opportunities for learning and growth. They encourage their teams to adopt the same mindset, creating a culture that values continuous improvement and innovation.

4. Build a Supportive Network

Resilient leaders recognize the importance of building a supportive network of mentors, peers, and advisors. They seek guidance and support from others, learning from their experiences and insights.

5. Lead with Purpose

Central to resilient leadership is leading with purpose. Resilient leaders communicate a clear vision and mission, aligning their teams' efforts with the organization's goals. They inspire their teams by exemplifying resilience in their actions and decisions.

6. Foster Adaptability

In the face of uncertainty and change, resilient leaders foster adaptability within their organizations. They encourage experimentation and risk-taking, recognizing that innovation often stems from trying new approaches.

7. Promote Learning and Development

Resilient leaders prioritize learning and development within their organizations. They invest in their teams' skill development, providing opportunities for training and upskilling.

Resilient leadership is a transformative force that propels organizations toward success in the face of adversity. By embodying traits such as vision, emotional intelligence, adaptability, and a growth mindset, leaders can create a resilient culture that empowers their teams to overcome challenges and thrive. The Resilient Leadership Framework serves as a guide for leaders to develop their resilience and inspire their teams to do the same. As leaders cultivate resilience within themselves and their organizations, they pave the way for a brighter and more prosperous future.

Resilient Leadership Matrix

Thriving in the Crucible

The Resilient Leadership Matrix is a cutting-edge and visionary framework that equips leaders with the dexterity to thrive in the crucible of modern challenges. It weaves together six dynamic dimensions, crafting a mosaic of innovation and fortitude that propels leaders and their organizations to new heights.

1. Visionary Prowess: The bedrock of the Resilient Leadership Matrix is visionary prowess. Leaders with visionary acumen possess an uncanny ability to articulate a compelling and audacious vision that ignites the passions of their teams. They paint vibrant tapestries of the future and rally their followers with fervour.

2. Emotional Alchemy: At the heart of resilience lies emotional alchemy—the art of transforming emotions into powerful catalysts for positive change. Resilient leaders master this skill, transmuting fear into courage, doubt into conviction, and setbacks into stepping stones towards triumph.

3. Adaptive Symphony: Resilient leaders are the conductors of an adaptive symphony, orchestrating harmonious collaboration between teams and departments. They embrace diversity, fostering a culture that cherishes uniqueness, innovation, and constant evolution.

4. Self-Discovery Nexus: The Resilient Leadership Matrix hinges on the self-discovery nexus - a profound journey of introspection that unearths a leader's authentic self. Here, leaders gain unparalleled clarity of their strengths and limitations, empowering them to lead with unwavering conviction.

5. Cultivated Resilience: Akin to a rare flower, resilience blooms through careful cultivation. Resilient leaders cultivate an environment that nourishes tenacity, growth, and agility. They nurture a culture of continuous learning, experimentation, and resilience-building.

6. Bold Ascent: At the apex of the Resilient Leadership Matrix stands the bold ascent-a daring leap into uncharted territories. Resilient leaders embrace uncertainty, fearlessly venturing into unexplored realms, and forging new pathways to success.

The Resilient Leadership Matrix is a masterpiece of innovation and adaptability. Each dimension interlaces with the others, amplifying the leader's impact and creating an organizational ecosystem that thrives on change, disruption, and transformation. With this ingenious matrix as their guide, leaders triumphantly navigate the tempests of the modern world, forging an indomitable legacy of resilience and greatness.

"
ENTREPRENEURSHIP:
BOUNCING BACK WITH BUSINESS BRILLIANCE!"

13 Entrepreneurial Resilience

In the fast-paced world of entrepreneurship, the journey is filled with exhilarating highs and daunting lows. Aspiring entrepreneurs embark on a roller-coaster ride, where unanticipated twists and turns are an inherent part of the landscape. In the face of uncertainty and ever-evolving challenges, resilience becomes the compass that guides them through the storm.

Every entrepreneur has a unique story, a tale of passion, innovation, and audacity. It is a story of taking risks, daring to dream, and embracing the unknown with unwavering determination. The path to success is not always smooth; hurdles and setbacks are inevitable. But what sets apart triumphant entrepreneurs from the rest is their ability to bounce back, learn from failures, and emerge stronger and more tenacious than ever before.

In this chapter, we delve into the world of entrepreneurial resilience – a trait that fuels creativity, adaptability, and resourcefulness. Here, we explore how successful entrepreneurs turn obstacles into stepping stones, leveraging their indomitable spirit to carve out a niche in the competitive business landscape.

The Gritty Entrepreneurial Spirit

Entrepreneurship demands more than just a grand vision; it demands an unwavering commitment and relentless determination. It requires the unyielding passion to transform ideas into reality. The grit to withstand the storms that come their way, for it is not just about building a business; it is about building an empire. Entrepreneurs walk a tightrope of uncertainties, where each decision holds the power to shape their destiny.

Here, we shed light on the audacious spirit that fuels entrepreneurs to take risks, challenge conventions, and persevere despite all odds. We explore real-life stories of entrepreneurs who transformed obstacles into opportunities, showcasing their determination and resilience in the face of adversity.

Navigating the Entrepreneurial Ecosystem

The entrepreneurial journey is not a solitary pursuit; it thrives on collaboration, networking, and harnessing opportunities. In this section, we unravel the importance of building a robust network, forging strategic partnerships, and leveraging the entrepreneurial ecosystem to grow and prosper.

Entrepreneurs often find themselves at crossroads, unsure of which path to tread. Here, we present insights into the art of making sound decisions, seeking guidance from mentors, and learning from experienced entrepreneurs who have braved similar challenges. We also delve into the significance of adapting to market dynamics, staying attuned to customer needs, and evolving in sync with the changing times.

Resilience through Innovation and Adaptation

Innovation is the heartbeat of entrepreneurship, and adaptability is the lifeblood that sustains it. In this section, we explore the art of disruption, and how entrepreneurs foster a culture of innovation to stay ahead of the curve. We unravel the transformative power of adapting to technological advancements and market disruptions.

Here, we explore how successful entrepreneurs defy conventional norms, reinvent their businesses, and create a niche for themselves in an ever-evolving world. We present case studies of start-ups that capitalized on the winds of change, pivoted their strategies, and emerged as industry leaders.

The Power of Positive Leadership

At the core of every successful entrepreneurial venture lies a leader with a vision that inspires, motivates, and empowers the team. In this section, we explore the essence of positive leadership and how it fosters a culture of resilience within an organization.

We delve into the qualities that make a leader stand out and the impact of their actions on the morale and productivity of the team. We showcase real-life stories of entrepreneurs who led their teams with grace, empathy, and the courage to make difficult decisions.

Thriving on the Entrepreneurial Edge

Entrepreneurship is a thrilling journey, but it comes with its share of stress and burnout. In this section, we address the importance of self-care, well-being, and mental resilience. We explore how entrepreneurs balance the demands of their work with personal life, and the significance of maintaining a healthy work-life integration. Here, we present practical strategies to manage stress, build resilience, and nurture a positive mindset that helps entrepreneurs maintain their edge while navigating the challenges of the entrepreneurial world.

Turning Failure into a Stepping Stone

Every entrepreneur encounters failure at some point in their journey. However, what sets apart the resilient ones is their ability to rise from the ashes and turn failure into a stepping stone towards success. In this section, we explore the art of learning from failure, embracing setbacks as valuable lessons, and using them as a springboard for growth.

We delve into the stories of entrepreneurs who faced failures but emerged stronger, wiser, and more determined to achieve their goals. Their journey demonstrates that failure is not a dead-end but a detour towards success.

The Resilient Entrepreneur's Mindset

The chapter culminates in exploring the mindset that distinguishes resilient entrepreneurs from the rest. We unravel the psychology behind the entrepreneurial spirit, the determination to persevere, and the unwavering faith in their vision.

We explore the power of optimism, gratitude, and the ability to see opportunities in every challenge. We showcase how successful entrepreneurs harness the power of positive thinking to overcome obstacles and shape their destinies.

We will celebrate the spirit of entrepreneurship and the unwavering resilience that propels them to new heights. The journey of an entrepreneur is an adventure like no other – a tale of courage, innovation, and the undying spirit to forge a brighter future. Resilient entrepreneurs inspire us to dream big, persist through the toughest storms, and celebrate every milestone along the way.

Navigating Business Challenges

In the realm of entrepreneurship, challenges are as inevitable as they are diverse. From financial constraints and fierce competition to unforeseen market shifts and global crises, entrepreneurs must navigate a maze of obstacles to sustain and grow their businesses. In this section, we delve into the art of resilient problem-solving, examining how successful entrepreneurs overcome adversities with determination and ingenuity.

1. Adapting to Market Turbulence

Businesses exist in a dynamic and ever-changing market landscape. Successful entrepreneurs have an inherent ability to adapt to market turbulence, recognizing that change is the only constant. They understand that the key to resilience lies in anticipating market shifts and seizing new opportunities.

Take the example of Akshay, a young entrepreneur who started a tech-based delivery service in India. When the COVID-19 pandemic hit, his business faced significant challenges due to lockdowns and movement restrictions. Instead of giving in to despair, Akshay swiftly pivoted his business model, partnering with local grocery stores to deliver essential items to people in need. This agile response not only kept his business afloat but also earned him the trust and loyalty of customers in the community.

2. Building Strategic Alliances

In the competitive business world, alliances play a pivotal role in driving growth and expanding market reach. Resilient entrepreneurs understand the value of strategic partnerships and collaborations, which can strengthen their position in the market and unlock new opportunities.

Consider the case of Rina and Sanjay, co-founders of a sustainable fashion brand in London. Despite facing tough competition from established players, they focused on building collaborations with local artisans and eco-friendly suppliers. This not only helped them create unique, eco-conscious products but also amplified their brand's mission. Through their strategic alliances, they were able to tap into a broader audience that appreciated their commitment to sustainability, leading to significant business growth.

3. Embracing Innovation and Technology

In today's digital age, innovation and technology are catalysts for growth and resilience. Savvy entrepreneurs leverage technological advancements to streamline operations, enhance customer experiences, and stay ahead of the curve.

Take the example of Divya, who runs a health and wellness startup in Delhi. Realizing the potential of telehealth services, she integrated virtual consultations into her platform, providing personalized health advice to customers across the country. This innovative approach not only expanded her business's reach but also ensured continuity of services during the pandemic when in-person consultations were restricted.

4. Fostering a Resilient Company Culture

A resilient company culture is the foundation of a thriving business. Entrepreneurs who prioritize employee well-being, foster a positive work environment, and empower their teams create an ecosystem that thrives in the face of challenges.

Consider the case of Anuj, founder of a tech start-up in Bengaluru. Anuj believed that nurturing a culture of open communication and innovation would drive his company's success. He encouraged his employees to voice their ideas and opinions freely, fostering a collaborative and inclusive work environment. This employee-centric approach not only boosted creativity but also bolstered employee loyalty, helping his company attract and retain top talent.

5. Financial Prudence and Risk Management

Financial stability is crucial for business resilience. Entrepreneurs who manage finances prudently, anticipate risks, and build contingency plans are better equipped to weather storms.

One such entrepreneur is Varun, who started a restaurant chain in Mumbai. Aware of the volatile nature of the food industry, Varun made it a priority to maintain a robust financial strategy. He secured lines of credit, built an emergency fund, and closely monitored cash flow. When the pandemic hit, Varun's preparedness allowed him to navigate the crisis, ensuring that his business survived and thrived once restrictions eased.

6. Leveraging Customer Insights

Customers are the lifeblood of any business, and successful entrepreneurs keenly understand their needs and preferences. By leveraging customer insights and feedback, entrepreneurs can adapt their products and services to meet evolving demands.

Consider the example of Meena, who founded an e-commerce platform in Hyderabad. Through meticulous customer surveys and data analysis, Meena identified a gap in the market for personalized, sustainable fashion. Armed with these insights, she curated a collection of eco-friendly clothing, resonating with environmentally conscious customers and establishing her brand as a go-to for conscious consumers.

Resilience in Crisis Management

Crisis management is a critical skill that separates resilient entrepreneurs from the rest. They proactively anticipate crises, have a clear action plan in place, and lead with transparency and empathy when facing challenges.

An example is the story of Raj, who runs a travel agency in Jaipur. When a natural disaster struck a popular tourist destination, Raj's business took a hit due to cancelled bookings and safety concerns. However, he swiftly mobilized resources to assist affected communities, demonstrating his commitment to responsible tourism. This proactive approach not only earned him the trust of customers but also garnered positive media attention, helping him recover from the setback.

Innovating and Adapting

In the ever-changing landscape of business, entrepreneurs must possess the innate ability to innovate and adapt. They understand that to remain relevant and competitive, they must constantly evolve and stay ahead of the curve. Innovation and adaptability are key pillars of entrepreneurial resilience, allowing visionaries to navigate through challenges and embrace opportunities with an unyielding spirit.

Meet Rahul, a visionary founder of a tech startup based in Bangalore. As he embarked on his entrepreneurial journey, Rahul quickly realized that the business world was a dynamic and unpredictable place. To succeed, he knew that he had to be prepared to embrace change and think outside the box.

In the early stages of his venture, Rahul faced fierce competition in the market. His innovative product was well-received by customers, but as the industry evolved, he sensed a shift in consumer preferences towards more sustainable and eco-friendly options. Recognizing the need to adapt, Rahul took a leap of faith and decided to pivot his business strategy.

He embarked on a journey of extensive research and development, exploring sustainable materials and eco-friendly manufacturing processes. It was a challenging endeavour, but Rahul's tenacity and belief in the potential of sustainable practices fuelled his determination. After months of hard work, he successfully launched an eco-friendly version of his product, setting his brand apart from competitors and attracting a growing base of environmentally conscious consumers.

The strategic innovation not only boosted Rahul's business growth but also reinforced his position as an industry trailblazer. His ability to adapt to evolving market trends not only secured the future of his startup but also inspired his team to embrace change and continue innovating.

Rahul's story exemplifies the essence of entrepreneurial resilience. It's not just about weathering the storm but also about seizing opportunities that arise amidst uncertainty. Entrepreneurial resilience is the foundation on which business leaders build success, enabling them to stay nimble and responsive to the changing needs of their customers and the market.

Innovation and adaptation go hand in hand. As entrepreneurs continuously innovate, they discover new ways to address challenges, streamline operations, and deliver superior value to their customers. By incorporating fresh perspectives and groundbreaking ideas, they can create cutting-edge solutions that revolutionize industries and spark societal change.

Adaptability, on the other hand, requires the flexibility to adjust strategies and embrace change when needed. It is the art of staying open-minded, recognizing market shifts, and being agile in response to emerging trends. By cultivating a culture of adaptability within their organizations, entrepreneurs empower their teams to face change with optimism, turning obstacles into stepping stones for progress.

The ability to innovate and adapt isn't confined to product development or market strategies; it also extends to fostering a resilient and dynamic workforce. Successful entrepreneurs understand the value of investing in their team's growth and well-being.

In the face of challenges, they nurture a culture of creativity and problem-solving, encouraging employees to contribute their ideas and perspectives. This collaborative environment not only fuels innovation but also boosts employee morale and engagement.

Entrepreneurs also understand the significance of investing in their team's skill development. They encourage continuous learning, providing employees with opportunities to enhance their capabilities and stay abreast of industry trends. This approach not only equips the workforce to tackle challenges head-on but also fosters loyalty and retention.

Innovation and adaptability are also closely intertwined with risk-taking. As entrepreneurs venture into uncharted territories, they are well aware that risk and uncertainty come hand in hand. However, they recognize that calculated risks are essential for growth and progress.

The willingness to take risks often leads to breakthrough moments that can redefine the trajectory of a business. Such leaps of faith have propelled entrepreneurs to achieve extraordinary feats, leading their organizations to new heights of success.

Embracing innovation and adaptability is an ongoing journey that requires continuous self-reflection and a growth mindset. As entrepreneurs embrace a never-ending pursuit of excellence, they understand that staying relevant in a dynamic world requires continuous evolution.

To cultivate a resilient and forward-thinking mindset, entrepreneurs draw inspiration from diverse sources. They seek inspiration from thought leaders and innovators across industries, attending conferences and networking events to exchange ideas and insights.

Additionally, entrepreneurs are keen observers of their surroundings. They draw inspiration from the world around them, exploring art, culture, and nature to spark creativity and ingenuity.

"Innovating and Adapting" showcases the vital role of these attributes in the entrepreneurial journey. The ability to innovate empowers entrepreneurs to create ground breaking solutions, while adaptability ensures their resilience in the face of change.

Entrepreneurial resilience is not just about survival; it's about embracing opportunities, challenging the status quo, and leaving a lasting impact on the world. By fostering a culture of innovation, adaptability, and calculated risk-taking, entrepreneurs set the stage for a future of endless possibilities and unyielding success.

Resilience in Start-Up Culture

In the town of Jaipur, India, a group of passionate young entrepreneurs came together to create "EcoServe," a start-up with a mission to revolutionize waste management and promote sustainable living. Their journey was a testament to the power of resilience in the face of adversity.

EcoServe's founders faced numerous challenges right from the start. Securing funding was a major hurdle as investors were hesitant to back a start-up focused on waste management, considering it an unconventional and risky venture. Undeterred, the founders pooled their limited resources and embraced the "bootstrap" approach, learning to do more with less.

The team worked relentlessly to develop innovative waste management solutions that catered to the unique needs of the community in Jaipur. They faced scepticism and resistance from local authorities and residents, who were apprehensive about adopting new waste disposal methods.

Instead of backing down, EcoServe's founders used these challenges as opportunities to educate and raise awareness about the importance of sustainable waste management. They organized workshops, conducted door-to-door campaigns, and engaged with the community to build trust and support for their cause.

As word spread about EcoServe's impactful work, they began receiving recognition and support from various organizations and government bodies. With growing momentum, they secured funding and expanded their operations to neighbouring towns, where they continued to make a significant impact on waste management practices.

Through perseverance, adaptability, and a deep commitment to their vision, EcoServe not only transformed waste management in Jaipur but also inspired similar initiatives in other parts of India. Their journey showcased the resilience and determination that is often required to drive change and create a meaningful impact in the world.

The story of EcoServe reminds us that resilience is not just about surviving; it's about thriving despite the odds and transforming challenges into stepping stones towards a brighter and more sustainable future. In the start-up culture, where uncertainty and obstacles are part of the journey, resilience is the driving force that propels entrepreneurs forward, turning dreams into reality.

"
FLEXIBILITY IN BODY AND MIND LEADS TO A
RESILIENT SPIRIT – BEND, BUT NEVER BREAK. "

14 The Resilient Body and Mind

In the pursuit of resilience, we often focus on external challenges and hardships, forgetting that our true strength lies within – in the union of our body and mind. Just like a symphony, the harmonious connection between the physical and mental realms creates a powerful and resilient force that can weather any storm.

Our bodies are temples, housing the essence of our existence, and our minds are like gardeners, nurturing the seeds of our thoughts and emotions. To cultivate resilience, we must treat both with care, wisdom, and love.

As we journey into Chapter 14, "The Resilient Body and Mind," we embark on a exploration of the interconnectedness between our physical well-being and mental fortitude. Here, we delve into the age-old wisdom that reveals how nurturing the body and mind empowers us to overcome life's challenges and thrive amidst adversities.

Within these pages, we shall traverse the landscapes of ancient wisdom, modern science, and timeless practices, uncovering the secrets to a resilient body and mind. Let us bask in the light of wisdom and awaken the innate power within us all.

The Sanctuary of the Body

In this opening section, we explore the body's sanctity and how it serves as the foundation of resilience. We discover how our daily habits, nutrition, and physical well-being influence our mental strength. Drawing from ancient traditions and modern research, we shall gain insights into nurturing a healthy body, thus creating a firm groundwork for mental resilience.

The Mind's Garden

Next, we delve into the intricacies of the mind, the powerful creator of our reality. Through mindfulness practices, meditation, and cultivating positive thoughts, we shall witness the mind's transformative potential. By understanding the delicate balance between the conscious and subconscious, we learn to harness the mind's energy for resilience and growth.

The Dance of Body and Mind

Here, we witness the enchanting dance between the body and mind. We shall discover how the mind's influence shapes our physical well-being, and conversely, how the body's vitality nurtures our mental health. Embracing this holistic approach, we begin to master the art of resilience, where each step and thought harmoniously synchronize to create an unbreakable spirit.

Tapping into the Power of Breath

Breath, the essence of life, is a potent tool for resilience. In this section, we explore the ancient practices of breathwork and pranayama, which facilitate healing, reduce stress, and instill clarity of mind. As we embark on this journey of mindful breathing, we uncover the key to unlocking our inner reservoir of strength.

The Alchemy of Mindfulness

Mindfulness, the art of living in the present moment, holds the key to transcending life's challenges. Here, we learn to cultivate mindfulness in every facet of our lives, from mundane tasks to transformative moments. By being fully present, we create a sanctuary for our soul to rest and rejuvenate, nourishing our resilience from the core.

The Resilient Mindset

In this section, we dive into the ocean of the mind and explore the foundation of a resilient mindset. Through the power of gratitude, positive affirmations, and reframing adversity, we gain the tools to transform challenges into opportunities. By embracing a resilient mindset, we become the architects of our destiny.

Unleashing the Inner Healer

Within us lies an innate healer – a source of boundless potential and resilience. In this section, we unveil the inner healer's power through practices such as visualization, self-compassion, and forgiveness. By connecting with this intrinsic force, we heal wounds, renew our spirit, and thrive amidst the storms of life.

The Symphony of Resilience

As we near the conclusion of this chapter, we witness the symphony of resilience – a grand crescendo of body, mind, and soul in perfect harmony. Through the integration of ancient wisdom and modern practices, we find ourselves equipped with the wisdom to navigate life's challenges with grace and tenacity.

"The Resilient Body and Mind," we unravel the power of wisdom that empowers us to unleash the true potential of our body and mind. Together, let us embark on this transformative journey to forge a lasting resilience that embraces life's adversities with open arms and emerges stronger, wiser, and more vibrant than ever before.

The Mind-Body Formula

Innovative Approach to

Physical Fitness and Mental Health

In the pursuit of resilience, we often find ourselves focusing solely on either physical fitness or mental well-being. However, true resilience lies in the synergy of both - the intricate dance between the body and mind that creates a powerful force to overcome life's challenges. Welcome to an innovative approach to physical fitness and mental health, where we unravel the Mind-Body Formula.

Section 1: The Mind-Body Connection

To embark on this transformative journey, we must first understand the profound connection between the body and mind. Ancient wisdom and modern research alike affirm that our physical health directly impacts our mental well-being, and vice versa. In this section, we delve into the intricate neural pathways and biochemical reactions that bind our physical and mental states, revealing the secrets to unlocking resilience.

Section 2: The Mind-Body Formula Unveiled

Drawing from the wisdom of spiritual masters, neuroscientists, and fitness experts, we unveil the Mind-Body Formula - a unique and innovative approach to fostering resilience. The formula emphasizes that physical fitness and mental health are not disparate realms but interwoven aspects of our being. By nurturing both, we create a solid foundation for resilience.

Section 3: Movement as Medicine

Traditional exercise regimens can sometimes feel monotonous and uninspiring. In this section, we explore an innovative approach to movement - one that goes beyond routine workouts and embraces the joy of physical expression. From dance therapy to mindful walks in nature, we discover the therapeutic power of movement in elevating both physical fitness and mental health.

Section 4: The Power of Mindful Exercise

Mindfulness, the practice of being fully present, has gained immense popularity in recent years. In this section, we explore the intersection of mindfulness and physical fitness. Through practices like yoga, tai chi, and qigong, we learn to cultivate a deep mind-body connection, enhancing our resilience by calming the mind and energizing the body.

Section 5: Nourishing the Mind, Nourishing the Body

A well-nourished body supports a resilient mind. This section delves into the innovative world of brain-boosting foods and their impact on mental health. From superfoods to mindful eating practices, we uncover the power of nutrition in fortifying our resilience from within.

Section 6: The Resilience Workout

Welcome to the Resilience Workout - a ground breaking blend of physical exercises and mental exercises. In this section, we combine innovative fitness routines with mindfulness practices, designed to strengthen the body and sharpen the mind. As we embark on this transformative journey, we witness the profound effects of the Mind-Body Formula in action.

Section 7: The Mind-Body Reset

Life's challenges can often leave us feeling depleted and overwhelmed. This section presents the Mind-Body Reset - a series of practices to recharge and rejuvenate. Through deep breathing techniques, guided imagery, and progressive relaxation, we restore the balance between the body and mind, fostering resilience and clarity of purpose.

Section 8: The Journey of Self-Discovery

Resilience is not solely about overcoming external challenges; it is also a journey of self-discovery. In this final section, we explore the transformative power of self-reflection and introspection. By understanding our unique strengths, weaknesses, and passions, we cultivate a profound sense of self-awareness that forms the bedrock of resilience.

The Mind-Body Formula transcends conventional notions of physical fitness and mental health, offering a revolutionary approach to resilience. As we integrate movement, mindfulness, and nourishment, we witness the remarkable transformation that unfolds within us. This chapter invites you to embrace the Mind-Body Formula, empowering you to forge a path of resilience, vitality, and self-discovery like never before. Together, let us embark on this journey of integrated well-being, unlocking the true potential of the Mind-Body connection.

The Science of Resilience

Unlocking the Secrets of Inner Strength

Welcome to the captivating world of the science of resilience. In this chapter, we will embark on a fascinating journey to explore the intricate workings of resilience from a scientific perspective. As we delve into cutting-edge research from various disciplines, we will uncover the underlying mechanisms that drive resilience and discover how we can cultivate this vital trait in our lives.

The Resilient Brain - Adapting and Rewiring

The human brain is a marvel of adaptability. Neuroscientists have uncovered the phenomenon of neuroplasticity, the brain's ability to reorganize itself by forming new neural connections. This remarkable feature allows the brain to adapt and reshape in response to experiences, including adversity.

Research has shown that resilience is closely tied to neuroplasticity. Individuals with higher levels of resilience exhibit enhanced neural connectivity in regions associated with emotional regulation and cognitive control. By understanding the brain's adaptability, we can actively engage in practices that promote neural rewiring and foster resilience.

The Neurochemistry of Resilience - A Symphony of Hormones

The neurochemistry of resilience is a symphony of hormones and neurotransmitters that influence our emotional responses and coping mechanisms. Cortisol, the stress hormone, plays a central role in our fight-or-flight response to stress. However, chronic stress can lead to an imbalance in cortisol levels, affecting our resilience.

On the other hand, neurotransmitters like serotonin, dopamine, and oxytocin are essential for emotional well-being and social bonding. Maintaining a healthy balance of these chemicals is crucial for building resilience and effectively navigating challenges.

The Resilient Mind-Body Connection

The mind and body are intricately connected, and their synergy significantly impacts our resilience. Research has shown that mindfulness practices and relaxation techniques can positively influence both mental and physical health.

Mindfulness meditation, yoga, and deep breathing exercises have been linked to reduced stress and improved emotional regulation. When we cultivate this mind-body connection, we equip ourselves with a powerful tool to cope with adversity and maintain inner equilibrium.

The Power of Belief

Psychologist Carol Dweck's groundbreaking work on the growth mindset reveals the power of our beliefs in shaping our resilience. Embracing a growth mindset means viewing challenges as opportunities for learning and personal growth, rather than fixed limitations.

By adopting a growth mindset, we can develop a more optimistic outlook on life, cultivate perseverance, and embrace resilience as a dynamic quality. This transformative belief in our own potential empowers us to overcome setbacks and thrive in the face of adversity.

The Resilient Social Network - Building Supportive Bonds

Humans are social beings, and our social connections have a significant impact on our resilience. Strong social support acts as a buffer against stress and enhances our ability to cope with life's challenges.

Nurturing meaningful relationships, fostering empathy, and building a supportive network are essential components of resilience. By surrounding ourselves with positive influences, we create a safety net that bolsters our inner strength during trying times.

We have unlocked a treasure trove of insights into this vital trait. From the adaptability of the brain to the orchestration of neurochemicals and the mind-body connection, resilience is a complex phenomenon shaped by multiple factors.

By applying the knowledge gleaned from this scientific framework, we can proactively cultivate our resilience and thrive amidst life's uncertainties. Embrace the power of resilience and embark on a transformative journey towards unwavering inner strength and self-discovery. Remember, within you lies the potential to rise above challenges and forge a brighter future filled with resilience and triumph.

Holistic Approaches to Well-being

Introducing the Resilience Well-Being Index (RWI)

The Resilience Well-Being Index (RWI) is an innovative and comprehensive formula that assesses holistic well-being by considering multiple dimensions of human experience. This formula goes beyond traditional health indices and focuses on fostering resilience, emotional intelligence, and spiritual growth. The RWI aims to provide individuals, organizations, and communities with a practical tool to enhance overall well-being and cultivate resilience in the face of life's challenges.

The RWI Incorporates six essential dimensions, each representing a critical aspect of holistic well-being:

Emotional Resilience (ER)

This dimension evaluates an individual's ability to cope with and bounce back from emotional challenges. It considers factors like emotional intelligence, self-awareness, and the capacity to regulate emotions effectively.

Physical Health (PH)

Physical health is a cornerstone of overall well-being. The RWI assesses physical fitness, nutrition, and the maintenance of a healthy lifestyle to ensure individuals are equipped to face life's demands.

Mental Agility (MA)

Mental agility encompasses cognitive flexibility, problem-solving skills, and the ability to adapt to new situations. This dimension evaluates one's capacity to embrace change and approach challenges with an open mind.

Social Connection (SC)

Social connection plays a vital role in well-being. The RWI evaluates the depth and quality of social relationships, community engagement, and support networks to foster a sense of belonging and connection.

Purposeful Living (PL)

This dimension explores an individual's sense of purpose and meaning in life. It assesses alignment with core values, fulfilment of personal goals, and the pursuit of meaningful endeavours.

Spiritual Growth (SG)

Spiritual growth refers to the development of inner strength, resilience, and self-awareness. The RWI emphasizes mindfulness practices, meditation, and self-reflection to enhance spiritual well-being.

Calculating the RWI

Each dimension is scored independently, and the RWI is calculated as an average of the six scores. Participants receive a score between 0 and 100, indicating their level of overall well-being and resilience.

Using the RWI

The RWI serves as a powerful tool for individuals and organizations seeking to promote holistic well-being and resilience. It can be utilized for personal development, employee well-being programs, community initiatives, and policy-making at the societal level.

Benefits of the RWI

Comprehensive Evaluation: The RWI provides a holistic assessment of well-being, recognizing the interconnectedness of emotional, physical, mental, social, and spiritual dimensions.

Personalized Insights: Participants gain personalized insights into their strengths and areas for growth, empowering them to make informed decisions about their well-being journey.

Resilience Building: By focusing on resilience as a central theme, the RWI equips individuals with the tools to navigate challenges and setbacks with greater ease and adaptability.

Promoting Positive Change: The RWI can drive positive change at the individual and community levels, inspiring people to prioritize their well-being and support others in their journey.

The Resilience Well-Being Index (RWI) is a ground breaking formula that prioritizes resilience and comprehensive well-being. By recognizing the multifaceted nature of human experience, the RWI empowers individuals and organizations to foster a culture of well-being and thrive in the face of life's complexities. Embrace the RWI as a powerful tool on your journey to holistic well-being and resilience!

Lessons from the Dalai Lama

Let's discuss the wisdom of the Dalai Lama, exploring holistic approaches to well-being that encompass the mind, body, and soul. The Dalai Lama, a revered spiritual leader, has spent his life promoting compassion, mindfulness, and inner peace. His teachings offer invaluable insights into achieving true well-being, which goes beyond physical health to encompass emotional, mental, and spiritual flourishing.

Cultivating Compassion - The Heart of Well-being

The Dalai Lama's teachings emphasize the power of compassion as a foundation for well-being. Compassion is not only an essential aspect of human connection but also a force that nurtures our own emotional health. By practicing compassion towards ourselves and others, we foster a positive, nurturing environment that promotes well-being on both individual and collective levels.

Mindfulness and Inner Peace - The Keys to Mental Well-being

Mindfulness is another cornerstone of the Dalai Lama's teachings. By being fully present in the moment and observing our thoughts without judgment, we cultivate inner peace and mental well-being. The practice of mindfulness allows us to disengage from negative thought patterns, reduce stress, and improve our overall emotional resilience.

Embracing Impermanence - Finding Serenity in Change

The Dalai Lama often speaks about the impermanence of life. Embracing the transient nature of existence can free us from the fear of change and uncertainty. By recognizing that everything is impermanent, we learn to let go of attachments and find solace in the flow of life's ever-changing currents.

The Power of Gratitude - Cultivating a Positive Mindset

Gratitude is a transformative force that the Dalai Lama frequently highlights. By practicing gratitude, we shift our focus from what is lacking to what we already have, fostering a positive mindset and greater contentment. Gratitude allows us to find joy in the simple pleasures of life and enhances our overall sense of well-being.

Connecting with Nature - Healing the Soul

The Dalai Lama's teachings also emphasize the importance of connecting with nature to nurture our souls. Spending time in nature helps us to unplug from the hectic modern world, reconnect with our inner selves, and find solace in the beauty and tranquillity of the natural world.

The Art of Forgiveness - Liberating the Soul

Forgiveness is a powerful tool for healing and well-being. The Dalai Lama speaks of the transformative power of forgiveness, both for ourselves and others. Letting go of past grievances and finding compassion for those who have hurt us can liberate our souls and bring inner peace.

Cultivating Resilience - Facing Life's Challenges

The Dalai Lama's life story is a testament to resilience. His teachings emphasize the importance of developing inner strength and resilience to navigate life's challenges with grace and determination. By facing difficulties with courage and compassion, we can grow and evolve on our journey towards well-being.

The Dalai Lama's profound teachings offer us a roadmap to holistic well-being, guiding us to nurture our minds, bodies, and souls. From cultivating compassion and mindfulness to embracing impermanence and finding solace in nature, his wisdom inspires us to live a life filled with purpose and contentment.

By integrating the lessons from the Dalai Lama into our daily lives, we embark on a transformative journey towards greater well-being, inner peace, and resilience. Remember, well-being is a multifaceted journey, and each step we take towards cultivating holistic health brings us closer to the authentic and fulfilling life we seek. Let the teachings of the Dalai Lama be a guiding light on this profound voyage towards holistic well-being.

15 Mental Resilience

In the symphony of life, the mind plays the most intricate instrument. Chapter 15: Mental Resilience unravels the secrets of fortifying this instrument, as we explore the boundless potential of our thoughts and emotions. Through the rollercoaster of ups and downs, our minds hold the key to navigate through the storms, empowering us to emerge stronger, wiser, and more resilient.

Life presents us with an array of circumstances, both exhilarating and challenging. Yet, within the labyrinth of experiences, our mental resilience serves as the guiding compass, illuminating the path to harmony and contentment. This chapter unveils the transformative power of our thoughts, the resilience of our minds, and the profound strength we possess to transcend adversity.

To build an unyielding fortress of mental resilience, we begin by recognizing the raw potential that resides within us. Each thought, an architect shaping the blueprint of our reality, opens doors to unforeseen opportunities. This chapter unravels the art of understanding our thoughts, dissecting the intricacies that mold our perceptions, and harnessing the potency to redirect them for growth and healing.

As we tread the labyrinth of our minds, emotions guide us through the labyrinth of our hearts. Emotions, like the tides of an ocean, ebb and flow, each wave a mirror of our inner landscapes. This chapter dives deep into the ocean of emotions, teaching us to dance with the tides, navigate through storms, and cultivate a serene inner sea that remains steady amidst life's tempestuous waters.

Within the pages of this chapter lies the invitation to embrace the power of self-compassion. As we learn to extend a gentle hand to ourselves, we foster the resilience that blossoms from embracing our flaws and embracing our imperfections. This transformative journey guides us towards self-awareness and self-love, nurturing the seeds of resilience that will weather any storm.

Life's canvas is painted with colours of uncertainty, change, and unexpected turns. Resilience, the artist's brush, gives us the ability to reimagine our reality and create a masterpiece of adaptability. Through stories of triumph and resilience, this chapter urges us to approach change with curiosity and courage, weaving the threads of flexibility into the tapestry of our lives.

As we venture deeper into the realm of mental resilience, we encounter the strength in vulnerability. Like a lotus blooming from the depths of a muddy pond, vulnerability heralds the path to growth and transformation. This chapter explores the art of embracing vulnerability, transcending our fears, and unearthing the diamond beneath the pressure of life's challenges.

Mindfulness, the essence of this chapter, invites us to step into the present moment with unwavering attention. In a world of distractions, the practice of mindfulness enables us to be fully present and attuned to the rhythm of life. As we cultivate this art, we discover the resilience that arises from dwelling in the sacred space of now.

The chapters that precede have paved the way for an extraordinary revelation – the boundless potential of the human spirit. As we delve into the depths of our inner world, we uncover the power to rewrite our narratives, reframing adversity into catalysts for growth. This chapter showcases the indomitable spirit of the human soul and its capacity to bloom like a lotus in the face of adversity.

At the heart of mental resilience lies the power of reframing our perceptions. Through the lens of optimism and gratitude, we can find strength and beauty even in the most challenging circumstances. This chapter encourages us to change our perspective, unveiling the art of shifting our focus towards positivity and appreciation.

In the midst of life's battles, we forge resilience through the art of self-regulation. Harnessing the ability to respond rather than react, we empower ourselves to navigate through turmoil with poise and grace. This chapter delves into the science of emotional regulation, guiding us to master the balance between control and surrender.

As we traverse the chapters of our lives, we recognize that resilience blooms from interconnectedness. This chapter explores the power of community, the magic of human connections, and the strength that emerges when we stand together as one. Uniting our stories, we find solace and inspiration in the shared journey of resilience.

The dance of resilience and growth intertwines with our sense of purpose and meaning. This chapter beckons us to discover our passions, uncover our purpose, and embrace a life of authenticity. As we align our actions with our deepest values, we nurture the roots of resilience that anchor us through life's uncertainties.

The journey of mental resilience leads us to the gateway of transformation. Through the alchemy of healing, forgiveness, and letting go, we liberate ourselves from the shackles of the past. This chapter invites us to turn the pages of our history and rewrite the chapters with the ink of compassion and grace.

In the grand tapestry of resilience, spirituality weaves a sacred thread that uplifts and empowers. This chapter celebrates the beauty of faith, the wisdom of surrender, and the serenity of inner knowing. As we journey through the realms of spirituality, we embrace the resilience that arises from connecting to something greater than ourselves.

In the final strokes of this chapter, we stand at the precipice of revelation – the symphony of resilience playing its crescendo within us. This chapter summons us to embrace the depth of our humanity, the strength of our spirit, and the brilliance of our resilience.

Within the pages of Chapter 15: Mental Resilience, we unearth the transformative journey of our minds and hearts, harmonizing the symphony of resilience within. As we navigate through life's turbulence, we discover that the resilience we seek resides not in the external world but within the vastness of our inner landscape. With each chapter, we reclaim the power to rewrite our stories, cultivating the unyielding strength to rise, to thrive, and to forge a brighter future.

Breaking Through Limitations

Breaking through limitations is an extraordinary journey of transformation, a symphony of resilience that unfurls the depths of our inner fortitude. It is an expedition that requires dismantling the mental barriers of fear and self-doubt, revealing the remarkable strength that lies dormant within us. As we embark on this odyssey, we confront our fears head-on, embracing setbacks as stepping stones to success, and recognizing that discomfort and vulnerability are gateways to profound growth.

In this pursuit of breaking through limitations, we find that we are not alone. We discover the power of collaboration, drawing strength from like-minded individuals who uplift and empower us. Through resilience, we learn to adapt and navigate the ever-changing landscapes of life, transforming each challenge into an opportunity for growth and triumph. Our journey is unique, shaped by the contours of our experiences, and driven by an unyielding belief in our worthiness to embrace our authentic selves.

As we traverse this path of resilience, we come to understand that the journey is continuous, not a destination. It is an ongoing process of self-discovery, where we find purpose and meaning in our lives. Each obstacle we conquer becomes a testament to our strength, while each setback offers invaluable lessons and insights that fuel our growth. We begin to rewrite our narratives, crafting a tale of courage, determination, and resilience.

A crucial aspect of breaking through limitations is fostering a support network. Surrounding ourselves with individuals who believe in our potential and share in our aspirations becomes a wellspring of encouragement and inspiration. Together, we ascend the peaks of resilience, creating an empowering bond that propels us forward.

Within this transformative journey, we learn to trust our intuition, the quiet voice within that guides us to our true purpose. As we follow our inner compass, we find ourselves stepping into uncharted territories, unafraid of the unknown, and embracing the possibilities that lie ahead.

Breaking through limitations grants us access to a realm of infinite potential, where we dare to dream beyond the confines of what we once thought possible. The limitations we once perceived become stepping stones as we transcend our boundaries and expand our horizons. In this boundless expanse, we cultivate a spirit that seeks growth, seizes opportunities, and celebrates resilience.

Ultimately, breaking through limitations is not just an individual pursuit; it is a collective endeavour. As we share our triumphs and tribulations, we become part of a larger tapestry of resilience. Drawing inspiration from others' journeys, we discover that our stories are interconnected, and our victories become a source of encouragement for others.

In summary, breaking through limitations is a profound journey that emboldens us to embrace our true potential. It demands courage, resilience, and the unwavering belief in our worthiness. With each challenge we conquer, we emerge stronger, and with each setback, we gain wisdom. Collaboration with others and drawing inspiration from their journeys provides the support and empowerment needed to push forward. Trusting our intuition and rewriting our narratives lead us to a life teeming with endless possibilities. Breaking through limitations is not a solitary endeavor; it is a symphony of growth and self-discovery, guided by the resolute understanding that greatness resides within each of us.

Building Lasting Resilience Habits

Building lasting resilience habits is akin to constructing a solid foundation for an enduring fortress. It requires a strategic and innovative approach, one that harnesses the power of incremental steps to create a sustainable and transformative impact. In this section, we will explore a proven and successful framework for cultivating resilience habits that stand the test of time.

Step 1: Self-Awareness and Mindset Shift

The journey towards lasting resilience begins with self-awareness. Understanding our strengths, weaknesses, and triggers empowers us to make intentional choices in times of adversity. This process involves a mindset shift, where we transition from a victim mentality to one of empowerment. Embracing the belief that we have agency over our responses to challenges lays the groundwork for building lasting resilience habits.

Step 2: Goal Setting and Intention

With self-awareness as our compass, we set clear and actionable goals for cultivating resilience. These goals are driven by intention and align with our values and aspirations. By setting realistic and achievable milestones, we create a roadmap for progress and development.

Step 3: Daily Practices and Rituals

Consistency is the cornerstone of building lasting resilience habits. Incorporating daily practices and rituals that support our goals ensures that resilience becomes an integral part of our lives. These practices may include meditation, gratitude journaling, physical exercise, or moments of reflection.

Step 4: Embracing Failure as a Stepping Stone

In the pursuit of building resilience habits, setbacks are inevitable. Embracing failure as a stepping stone rather than a stumbling block allows us to learn and grow from our experiences. We recognize that resilience is not about avoiding challenges but about bouncing back stronger after facing them.

Step 5: Seeking Support and Mentorship

Resilience is not a solo endeavour; it thrives in a supportive ecosystem. Seeking guidance from mentors and peers who have cultivated lasting resilience habits offers valuable insights and encouragement. Collaborative environments nurture growth and provide a safety net during times of difficulty.

Step 6: Cultivating a Growth Mindset

A growth mindset is the fertile soil in which resilience habits take root and flourish. Embracing the belief that our abilities can be developed through dedication and hard work fuels our perseverance in the face of obstacles.

Step 7: Managing Stress and Building Emotional Intelligence

Resilience is not just about weathering storms but also about managing stress and emotions effectively. Developing emotional intelligence empowers us to navigate challenging situations with grace and composure.

Step 8: Adaptability and Flexibility

Resilience habits are not rigid; they adapt and evolve as we encounter new experiences and circumstances. Cultivating adaptability and flexibility enables us to navigate life's twists and turns with ease.

Step 9: Cultivating Positivity and Gratitude

Practicing positivity and gratitude amplifies the effects of resilience. Focusing on what we are grateful for and maintaining a positive outlook fosters an unwavering belief in our ability to overcome challenges.

Step 10: Review and Reassess

Building lasting resilience habits is an ongoing process. Regularly reviewing our progress and reassessing our goals ensures that we stay on track and continue to grow.

By following this innovative and successful framework, we pave the way for lasting resilience habits that infuse our lives with strength, courage, and grace. As we cultivate these habits, we become architects of our own resilience, constructing a foundation that can weather any storm and stand the test of time.

Embracing a Resilient Life

In the realm of fortitude and perseverance, there exists a sacred path that leads to the embodiment of a truly extraordinary life. This profound odyssey beckons us to embrace our innate strength, adaptability, and unwavering spirit. As we traverse this path, we weave a vivid memory of experiences, emotions, and lessons, creating a masterpiece that is uniquely ours. We set on an unparalleled exploration of the principles and practices that guide us in embracing a resilient life.

These words, like stars in the night sky, shine brightly, illuminating the way to an extraordinary existence.

1. Resilience is not merely surviving; it is thriving amidst the tempest, blooming in the harshest conditions, and transcending limitations.

2. Embrace the dance of fortitude; let it lead you through the highs and lows, for therein lies the symphony of life.

3. Like a phoenix rising from the ashes, resilience ignites the flames of hope and transformation.

4. In the crucible of adversity, resilience forges the steel of character, crafting a soul that is unbreakable and relentless.

5. The heart of resilience beats in sync with the rhythm of life, daring to dream and daring to conquer.

6. When life hurls its fiercest storms, resilience stands tall, anchored in the unyielding belief that we are destined for greatness.

7. Embrace the art of letting go, for in surrender lies the power to transcend the shackles of circumstance and emerge victorious.

8. In the tapestry of life, resilience threads the needle of courage, stitching together the moments that define us.

9. Every scar etched on our soul tells a story of resilience, where pain transformed into strength and vulnerability into wisdom.

10. Embrace your imperfections, for in their midst lies the brilliance of resilience, transcending limitations and illuminating the path to greatness.

11. Resilience is the compass that navigates us through life's labyrinth, illuminating the way forward with the light of hope.

12. When the world trembles, and shadows loom large, resilience is the beacon that guides us to the shores of triumph.

13. Embrace the ebb and flow of life, for resilience knows that every tide carries the promise of renewal and growth.

14. Like a lotus emerging from the mud, resilience blooms in the midst of adversity, radiating beauty and tenacity.

15. In the tapestry of resilience, vulnerability is the golden thread that weaves together the fabric of authenticity.

16. When darkness descends, and all seems lost, resilience whispers, "You are stronger than you know."

17. Embrace the power of vulnerability, for it is the gateway to resilience, where strength arises from the depths of the soul.

18. When life's storms rage, resilience stands firm, like an unwavering lighthouse guiding us to safe shores.

19. In the depths of despair, resilience kindles the flame of hope, igniting the spirit to rise and embrace life's challenges.

20. Embrace the dance of resilience, where each step becomes a testament to your unwavering spirit and indomitable will.

21. When faced with darkness, resilience becomes the North Star, guiding us through the night towards the promise of a brighter day.

22. In the crucible of adversity, resilience transforms wounds into wisdom, paving the way to a life of purpose and fulfilment.

23. Embrace the beauty of resilience, for it reveals the intricate masterpiece that emerges from life's trials and tribulations.

24. When the world challenges us, resilience reminds us that within us lies the strength to conquer and the power to rise.

25. In the tapestry of resilience, each thread is a testament to the human spirit's boundless capacity for growth and renewal.

26. Embrace the symphony of resilience, where every note played is a reflection of the soul's unwavering grace and strength.

These words, like a symphony of resilience, sing a song of hope, inspiration, and triumph, inviting us to embrace the extraordinary journey of a resilient life. May they resonate deeply within your heart, guiding you to unlock the dormant power of resilience and forge an extraordinary existence.

"Unseen Stars: A Journey of Resilience"

In the bustling city of New York, amidst the towering skyscrapers and the symphony of diversity, lived a young woman named Aria. She was born in a remote village in the Himalayas and had faced numerous challenges to reach the city that never sleeps. Aria's journey was not just about geographical distance but also about bridging cultural gaps and breaking barriers.

Growing up in a traditional village, Aria had a passion for science and dreamed of becoming a renowned astrophysicist. However, her dreams were met with scepticism and resistance from her conservative community, who believed that a woman's place was confined to the household.

Undeterred, Aria held on to her dreams with an unwavering determination. She sought solace in the night sky, gazing at the stars that seemed to hold the secrets of the universe. In those quiet moments, she found comfort and inspiration, as if the vastness of space was urging her to reach for the stars.

As fate would have it, Aria's talent and dedication caught the attention of an astrophysics professor from Columbia University. Impressed by her intellect and resilience, the professor offered her a scholarship to pursue her studies in the United States.

Aria's journey from her village to the bustling streets of New York was not without its challenges. She faced cultural shock, language barriers, and the weight of homesickness. Yet, her spirit remained unyielding, for she knew that every obstacle was an opportunity to grow.

In the hallowed halls of Columbia University, Aria found herself surrounded by some of the greatest minds in science. The diversity of the academic community mirrored the vibrancy of the city itself, and Aria felt a sense of belonging she had never known before.

With each passing day, Aria delved deeper into the mysteries of the cosmos. Her research on black holes and dark matter captured the attention of the scientific community, earning her recognition and respect.

But amidst the accolades and achievements, Aria faced a moment of doubt. The pressures of academia and the weight of her dreams seemed too much to bear. In her darkest hour, she gazed at the stars once more, seeking guidance and strength.

And then, like a celestial revelation, it dawned upon her that the resilience she had cultivated in her journey was the very force that could propel her forward. Aria realized that the universe itself was resilient, constantly evolving and adapting to the forces of nature.

With a renewed sense of purpose, Aria embraced her struggles as opportunities for growth. She started mentoring young women from diverse backgrounds, inspiring them to pursue their passions fearlessly. Aria's journey from a remote village to a leading scientist became a symbol of empowerment and transformation.

Her story transcended borders and cultures, captivating hearts and minds across the globe. Invitations poured in from various countries to share her journey, spreading the message of resilience, perseverance, and the pursuit of dreams.

Through Aria's extraordinary journey, the world learned that resilience knows no boundaries, that it can thrive even amidst the most diverse and challenging contexts. Her life became an ode to the human spirit's boundless potential to rise above adversity and soar to greater heights.

As we conclude this remarkable tale, let us remember Aria's journey and the profound lesson it holds—that resilience is a universal language that unites us all. Across oceans and cultures, amidst dreams and challenges, it is the force that propels us to embrace the extraordinary within ourselves.

So, dear reader, as you navigate the tapestry of life, let Aria's story be a guiding star, reminding you that within your heart lies the strength to overcome any obstacle and create an extraordinary life. For in the boundless expanse of the universe, each of us is a shining star, waiting to illuminate the world with the brilliance of resilience.

Dear Readers,

As I come to the end of this journey together, I am filled with profound gratitude and a sense of wonder. This book, "Unleashing Resilience: Embracing the Extraordinary," is a tapestry woven with inspiration from various sources—each thread representing a unique story of strength, courage, and perseverance.

First and foremost, I must express my heartfelt thanks to my mother, the guiding light in my life. Her unwavering support and belief in my dreams have been the foundation of my resilience. Her love and sacrifices have shown me the true meaning of strength, and I dedicate this book to her.

To every person I've encountered along the way, who has shared their struggles and triumphs, thank you for allowing me to witness the extraordinary resilience within you. Your stories have inspired me to dig deeper into the human spirit's incredible capacity to rise above adversity.

Life itself has been my greatest teacher, offering invaluable lessons that have shaped the words on these pages. It has taught me that resilience is not a trait reserved for the few; rather, it is a seed planted within all of us, waiting to blossom when nurtured with courage and determination.

I am humbled by the wisdom of those who have walked the path before us—leaders, thinkers, and visionaries who have gifted the world with their insights. Their ideas have enriched this book, and I am forever grateful for their contributions.

As I reflect on the writing journey, I must also acknowledge the profound influence of the divine. It is the belief in something greater than ourselves that fuels our resilience, knowing that we are part of a grand tapestry of interconnected lives.

Lastly, I bow to the beautiful souls who inhabit this planet—individuals who face unimaginable challenges yet embody resilience in its purest form. Your strength and resilience inspire me to strive for greater heights and continue spreading the message of hope.

As you turn the final page of this book, my hope is that it leaves an indelible mark on your heart. May you embrace the beauty of your own resilience and embark on a journey of self-discovery and empowerment.

Remember, dear reader, you hold within you the power to transform challenges into stepping stones and adversities into opportunities. Embrace your unique resilience, for it is the key that unlocks the door to an extraordinary life.

With heartfelt gratitude and love,

Vikas Parihar

9 789889 233818